The Router Table Book

The Router
Table Book

ERNIE CONOVER

The Taunton Press

BOOKS & VIDEOS

for fellow enthusiasts

First printing: November1994
Printed in the United States of America

A Fine Woodworking Book

Fine Woodworking® is a trademark of The Taunton Press, Inc.,
registered in the U.S. Patent and Trademark Office.

The Taunton Press, 63 South Main Street, Box 5506, Newtown,
CT 06470-5506

Library of Congress Cataloging-in-Publication Data

Conover, Ernie.
    The router table book / Ernie Conover.
       p. cm.
    "A Fine Woodworking book"—T.p. verso.
    Includes index.
    ISBN 1-56158-084-8
    1. Routers (Tools).   2. Workshops—Equipment and
supplies.   3. Joinery.   I. Title.
    TT203.5.C66   1994   94-24591
   684'.083—dc20   CIP

I dedicate this book to my wife, Susan, without whose help and encouragement I would never have written at all.

ACKNOWLEDGMENTS

Writing a technical book is a group effort! I extend special thanks to the following especially long-suffering individuals for their invaluable help: to Dave Keller and Matt Popik of Porter-Cable for engineering oversight and to Dave Hout, Al Russo of Vermont American, Chris Carlson of Bosch, Zach Etheridge of Highland Hardware, Dan and Linda Walter of Eagle America, Brad Witt of Woodhaven, and Mark Duginske for their deep knowledge of the router industry.

I would like to recognize the following individuals for their help in special areas: Rodger Gardner of Precision Metalsmiths (metallurgy oversight), Wayne Green, Larry Knapp of Formica Corp, Mike Hoag of the National Particleboard Association, Mark Schiefer of Delta, Mike Dunbar, Steve Spoon of Wisconsin Knife Works, Rick Schmidt of Porter-Cable, Terry Farmer of Carbide Alloys and Berry Blackburn of Sprayway. I also wish to thank the many other people, too numerous to list here, who offered their help and product information.

I would thank my editors, Helen Albert and Ruth Dobsevage, for bringing organization and clarity to this work. Finally, thanks to my wife and family for allowing me the time to do this book and for reviewing the manuscript.

CONTENTS

INTRODUCTION

The router is one of the most useful tools in the woodworking shop. In many ways it is to the modern woodworker what a plane was to yesterday's hand-tool woodworker. The router can profile an edge, make molding, cut all types of grooves, dadoes and fillisters, create mortise-and-tenon joints, make rule and door joints, cope any shape into end grain, do a multitude of pattern work and trim one surface flush to another—all tasks previously done by hand planes. While much of this work can be satisfactorily accomplished with a hand-held router, the full potential of the tool is realized only when it is mounted in a router table. The table allows operations and precision impossible with the hand-held router.

The router table is an inexpensive piece of equipment. Many of us already own the key component, a router, and router bits are reasonably priced and may be purchased as needed. Especially if it is shop made, a router table can be had for a fraction of the cost of other shop machines. In fact, the best router table you can obtain may be the one you build yourself. Unlike other tools, there is no sacrifice in quality with a home-built machine.

While many woodworkers have router tables, few use them to anything approaching their full potential. I think this is for a variety of reasons. For one thing, the router table has been the province of the home and small workshops, while industry uses other machines. Knowledge has not crossed over, more to lack of communication than anything. To be sure, there are many articles and books on the router and router table, but most fail to treat anything but very small-scale work, totally ignoring joinery operations and procedures.

In this book I will share the secrets of joinery with the router table. The emphasis will always be on safety and first-class results. Since the key to mastering the router table is a thorough understanding of setup, much space will be devoted to this subject. Remember, however, I can only give examples of typical setups. Setup is a way of thinking and not a prescribed doctrine. While the same general methods and procedures are used in all setups, they are used in different combinations and ways from job to job. Different workers might even set up the same job in quite different ways. By learning procedure, rather than dogmatic setups, you will be able to tackle all joinery problems (including the unusual) with speed, safety and confidence. Sit back, read on, and let's explore the router table together.

CHAPTER 1

Routers for Router Tables

Routers are at the heart of the router table, and selecting a router is one of the first decisions you need to make. In this chapter we'll have a look at various types of routers and some useful after-market accessories, as well as the basics of eye, ear and respiratory protection. Space precludes a detailed evaluation of specific routers, and since new models come on the market every few months, that sort of discussion would quickly become dated. Instead, I'll emphasize the design features you should look for in a router for your router table, so that you can make the best choice for your needs.

Types of Routers

The router was invented during World War I by Syracuse, New York, patternmaker R. L. Carter. He manufactured just shy of 100,000 of his ¼-hp routers before selling the design to the Stanley Company in 1929. Since then many other manufacturers have jumped on the bandwagon, and over the years routers became smaller and lighter but also more powerful and easier to adjust. Today's routers fall into two main categories: helical adjusting and plunge. Most manufacturers make

Selecting a router for your router table can be a daunting task, given the number of models on the market. Some of the factors to consider are the adjustment mechanism (helical vs. plunge), the horsepower rating and the style of collet design. Photo: Susan Kahn.

both types in two or three quality ranges. Light-duty "home-owner" routers, with a ¼-in. collet and as little as ¼ hp, sell for as little as $50. Commercial-duty routers have multiple collet sizes, better bearings and motor construction, and cost more. At the top end, industrial-duty routers have top-notch construction throughout and sell for $200 to $300. See Sources of Supply on pp. 114-116 for the addresses of some of the main router manufacturers.

Helical adjusting routers

Other than being much smaller and more powerful, today's helical adjusting routers resemble R. L. Carter's first router. In this design the motor screws into a helical slot in the body (see the drawing at left). Turning the motor raises and lowers the bit; a locking screw prevents the setting from drifting. In Carter's original design, the body had a thread of 16 threads per inch so that turning the motor within the base one full turn raised or lowered the bit $\frac{1}{16}$ in. This relatively fine thread allowed for precise adjustments, but setting the depth of cut was a slow process. Today most helical adjusting routers have a much coarser thread with a ring scale graduated in sixty-fourths of an inch, so the bit can be quickly raised and lowered in small increments (see the photo on the facing page). Helical adjusting routers are easy to operate, and the adjusting mechanism is nearly indestructible.

Many helical adjusting routers have motors with less than 2 hp, but nowadays more powerful 3-hp models are becoming available. With a ½-in. collet, a 1½-hp to 2-hp helical adjusting router can be quite suitable for many table operations. Although 2 hp is not sufficient power for large bits, it is adequate for small to medium sizes, including most panel door sets.

Some helical adjusting routers are fitted with speed control, which makes them even better for table work. As discussed on pp. 10-11, being able to reduce the speed of large cutters is a must, and a router that comes with speed control won't need an after-market unit.

I like to use helical adjusting routers for table work because I find them easier to adjust than plunge routers. One word of caution: Be sure to lock the motor before starting the router, or the motor can spin out of the base and go snarling about the floor. One problem with helical adjusting routers used in router tables is that the position of the

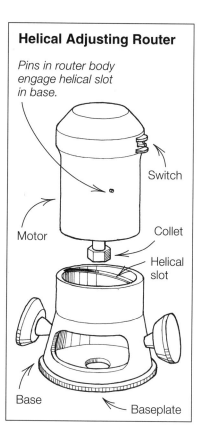

Helical Adjusting Router

Pins in router body engage helical slot in base.

Switch

Motor

Collet

Helical slot

Base

Baseplate

Most helical adjusting routers have a ⅟₆₄-in. ring scale that facilitates precise raising and lowering of the bit.

switch changes as the bit height is adjusted, so that one is never quite sure where it is. Feeling around blindly under a running router table is not the best idea, so bending over to look is necessary. Therefore a separate switch on the table is highly desirable.

Rack-and-pinion adjusting routers The rack-and-pinion system is a variation on the helical adjusting system. On rack-and-pinion adjusting routers, the motor has a rack machined in the side of it. A pinion gear in the base casting meshes with the rack and raises or lowers the motor when a knob is turned. In the past the system was quite popular, but today the only company I know of that still makes rack-and-pinion adjusting routers is Black & Decker. However, that router doesn't have enough horsepower for general router-table use. If you already own this rack-and-pinion router, you can use it in a router table, but only with small-diameter bits.

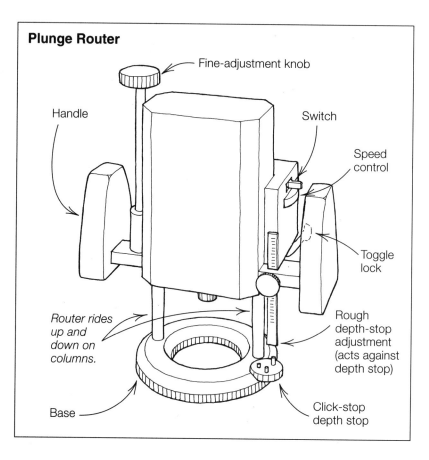

Plunge Router

Fine-adjustment knob

Handle

Switch

Speed control

Toggle lock

Router rides up and down on columns.

Rough depth-stop adjustment (acts against depth stop)

Base

Click-stop depth stop

Plunge routers

Many people think the plunge router was first introduced into this country by Japanese manufacturers, but that is far from the truth. R. L. Carter had a router with plunge features in his line in the early part of this century. Wherever it came from, the design has proved so popular that most manufacturers now offer one or more plunge routers in their line.

In a typical plunge router, the motor rides up and down on two columns rising out of the router base (see the drawing above). Settings are locked in place at the desired depth by a toggle lock. Springs in the columns maintain upward pressure against the motor so that the bit will naturally rise up out of the work when the toggle lock is released. In most plunge routers the toggle lock can be reached with the right or left index finger. When you place the router on the work, pull the toggle and press down, the bit will emerge from the base and enter the work. A depth stop arrests downward travel at the desired bit depth. With the plunge router, the switch is always just where you left it, regardless of the depth setting.

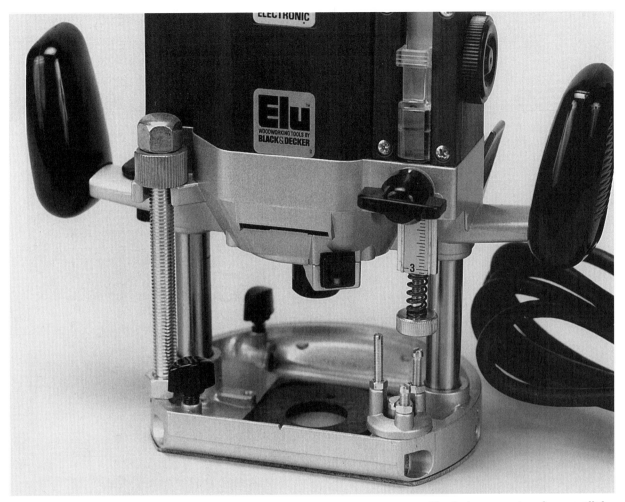

Most plunge routers have a click-stop mechanism for setting the depth of the cut. A threaded shaft and a set of nuts let you make fine height adjustments or lock a setting so that it cannot drift during a cut.

Most plunge routers have a rather sophisticated depth-stop mechanism (see the photo above). Click stops allow three or more progressively deeper depth settings to facilitate roughing and finishing cuts. Most plunge routers also have a threaded shaft with nuts to lock a depth setting so that it cannot change should the toggle accidentally be pulled.

A plunge router with 3 or more hp is very good for router-table use. Three horsepower will power any bits you are likely to use. Here too, speed control is a most desirable feature, in fact it is a must for large panel-raising bits (see pp. 66-67).

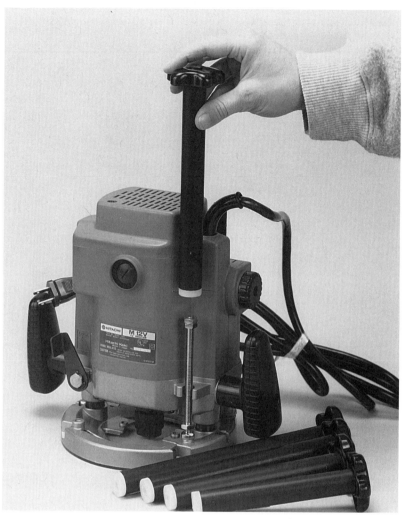

Depth-of-cut adjustment under the router table is more convenient if the nuts are replaced with an after-market router knob. On some routers, this knob is a standard item.

With plunge routers releasing the toggle and simply raising or lowering the motor is fine for coarse adjustment but not so good if you need to raise or lower a bit $\frac{1}{64}$ in. For this most people use the nuts on the threaded spindle. Since working under a table with a set of wrenches on a small set of nuts is cumbersome, to say the least, it is useful to replace the nut with an after-market router knob (see the photo above), which allows quick and easy height adjustment with one hand.

Choosing a Router

I am frequently asked what is the best router to buy for router-table work, and it's not an easy question to answer. Any router can be used in a table, but some are definitely better than others. Power is of course an important consideration, and how powerful your router needs to be depends largely on what type of work you plan to do. But power can be tricky to evaluate, because of the relationship of horse-power to amperage, as discussed on p. 10.

Don't be lured by power alone, for convenient features that make your router friendly to use every day are far more important than another amp or two. Pick the best machine you can afford and buy adequate horsepower, but above all look at features. I would much prefer a 3-hp router that I found easy to adjust to a $3\frac{1}{4}$-hp model that fought adjustment every sixty-fourth of the way. Other router features to consider include speed control and collet design.

Discerning differences in quality among competing routers can be difficult. Routers are mass-manufactured items and are designed around price points, so competing routers selling for about the same price will have about the same quality in their motors and bearings. Therefore, the buying decision comes down to features. Buy the router in the price range you can afford whose features appeal to you the most.

Table operations are much more demanding than hand-held work because you can force work into the bit, causing the motor to work harder than it should. In fact, some manufacturers stipulate that using their routers in tables voids the warranty. (One industry engineer I spoke with said that table mounting causes as much as eight times the warranty claims.) It's a good idea to check the manufacturer's warranty statement before you buy.

Buying a heavy-duty router certainly makes sense. If possible, buy an industrial-quality router and not a home-owner model, for the former will have ball-bearing construction and a high-quality motor while the latter may have sleeve bearings, which have more play in them and wear out more quickly. While most power-tool manufacturers offer a "professional" line of tools, only a few (among them Bosch, Hitachi, Makita, Porter-Cable and Skil) offer true industrial-duty tools.

Horsepower vs. amperage

One of the most confusing aspects of buying a router is evaluating claims of power. Power is listed in two ways: maximum horsepower and rated amperage. Maximum horsepower figures prominently in advertising and on the box. It represents the maximum horsepower the motor can develop and is determined through laboratory testing on a dynamometer. However, don't be too taken in by this figure, because a motor can maintain the maximum horsepower for only a short period of time without burning up. Maximum horsepower is useful primarily as a benchmark comparison among tools. But keep in mind that table operation can put demands on the motor that approach the maximum horsepower rating if wood is forced into the bit.

Rated amperage is a better predictor of router power than maximum horsepower. Rated amperage (which is listed on the tool's name plate) is defined as the amperage the tool can draw all day long without burning up; it is considerably less than the maximum amperage that would be drawn during the maximum horsepower test.

If you know the router's rated amperage value, you can use the following formula to calculate the approximate continuous horsepower your router will deliver in real working situations:

$$\frac{\text{Rated amperage x 120 volts}}{746} = \text{Approximate continuous horsepower}$$

In the formula, 120 volts is a constant (the standard line voltage in North America), and 746 is the number of watts in 1 hp. Approximate continuous horsepower is a much better basis for comparison among various routers than maximum horsepower, and is usually significantly less than the horsepower listed on the box.

For example, the Porter-Cable #7518 router (shown in the photo on p. 5), with a rated amperage of 15 amps, has an approximate continuous horsepower of 2.41, considerably less than the tool's advertised rating of $3\frac{1}{4}$ hp. This is still a very powerful tool, more than adequate for all types of router-table use.

Speed control

Traditionally routers were single-speed machines, running somewhere around 20,000 rpm. Today, however, many routers come equipped with speed control (see the photo on the facing page), which is a very desirable feature for router-table work, since large-

Built-in speed control lets you slow down the cutting speed for working with large-diameter cutters.

diameter cutters, such as panel-raising bits and large molding profile bits—must be run at lower speeds. Speed control lets you run bits at speeds as low as 8,000 rpm. For more on the relationship between bit diameter and speed, see p. 67.

Speed control built into the router is better than an after-market speed control that the router plugs into. Built-in speed controls are designed specifically for the needs of the router and typically have more sophisticated sensing electronics to monitor the motor's load and keep it running at a constant rpm. Also, built-in controls have passed independent laboratory testing, such as U.L. and C.S.A., along with the router, while an after-market speed control may not have undergone any testing whatsoever. Finally, built-in speed control gives you a true indication of how fast the bit is spinning. With an after-market control you have no way of knowing how exactly how much you are reducing the speed.

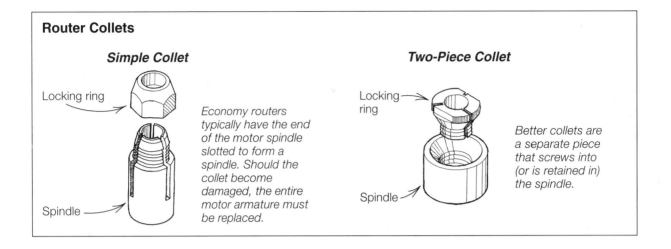

Router Collets

Simple Collet

Locking ring

Spindle

Economy routers typically have the end of the motor spindle slotted to form a spindle. Should the collet become damaged, the entire motor armature must be replaced.

Two-Piece Collet

Locking ring

Spindle

Better collets are a separate piece that screws into (or is retained in) the spindle.

Collet design

The collet, which holds the bit in the spindle, is a crucial component of any router. Since changing bits is such a common operation, an easy-to-use design is imperative. The most common sizes for collets are ¼ in. and ½ in., though you may also encounter metric-sized collets for use with metric-sized bits.

In North America a ½-in. collet router with interchangeable collets is your best investment for table operations. Happily, better ½-in. routers come today with both ¼-in. and ½-in. collets, and metric sizes can be ordered; the now almost defunct ⅜-in. collet size can also be special ordered.

At its simplest a collet is a metal tube that is partially slotted lengthwise (see the drawing above). A taper on the outside of the tube engages a mating taper in the spindle. A threaded locking ring, which screws onto (or into) the spindle, compresses the tube, which in turn grips the shank of the router bit. Cheap collets have only two slits; better collets have three or four. Economy routers (especially ¼-in. routers) often have the end of the spindle slit directly to form a collet. The problem with this design is that should the collet become damaged (a distinct possibility) the entire motor spindle and the armature around it have to be replaced. It is often cheaper to buy a new router.

Collets vary greatly both in their ease of use and in how well they grip the bit shank. Good collets do not require a lot of tightening to grip well, just mild to firm pressure on the wrench. Cheap collets often slip, no matter how much force is used in tightening. An idiosyncrasy of some collet designs is that when bits are being removed, the locking ring will spin free, but the bit is still gripped securely. If you con-

tinue to loosen the ring until a second resistance is felt, then further apply the wrench, the bit will come free. One of the best collets on the market, the Elu, works like this, and it's nothing to worry about.

Better routers have two-piece collets that slip into a bored opening machined in the end of the spindle. This design allows the use of interchangeable collets to accommodate bits of any size. Should a collet become damaged, it can easily be replaced.

With ½-in. collets another way to grip smaller-shank bits is with the use of an adapter bushing. As shown in the drawing at right, an adapter bushing is just a slit metal tube that slips into the ½-in. router collet. Better bushings have one or more partial slits, which make them more flexible so the force of the collet is more readily transmitted to the shank of the bit. How well an adapter bushing grips a bit depends on both the quality of the bushing itself and the collet it is used in. Often the bushing will take a set, so inserting and removing the bit shank becomes difficult. Because adapter bushings are prone to slippage and are burdensome to use, it's best to avoid them unless you have no other alternative.

Traditionally two wrenches are necessary for opening and closing the collet (see the photo above). One wrench grips two flats (or sometimes a hex on better routers) on the shaft just under the collet area, while the other tightens or loosens the locking ring. The task can be tedious, especially if wrenches of two sizes are required—you never seem to have the right wrench in the right hand. Some routers have shafts that lock, so to open or close the collet all you need is a wrench for the locking ring—this is a most desirable feature. Locking mecha-

Adapter Bushing

Adapter bushings let you use smaller-shank bits in a larger collet, but they are prone to slippage. It's best to use a collet of the proper size.

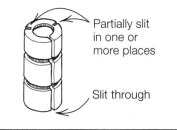

Partially slit in one or more places

Slit through

nisms range from a simple button that engages a hole in the shaft to a U-shaped toggle that amounts to a wrench but pivots over a hex on the end of the shaft when needed. The advantages of this system are that high torque can be applied, and the shaft is not weakened by a hole in or through it.

Router Accessories

Woodworking catalogs are loaded with accessories for the router. Two that directly relate to the use of the router in a table are after-market baseplates and switches.

After-market baseplates

Every router comes with a sturdy, low-friction plastic baseplate that allows the tool to slide easily on the work. These baseplates can be cut by a router bit, allowing modification to accommodate larger bits. Further, should the bit accidentally touch the baseplate, no harm is done. The baseplate often facilitates the mounting of guide bushings as well (see pp. 76-77).

For table operation, you usually remove the baseplate that comes with the tool and add a larger baseplate, which lets you mount the router in a rabbeted cutout in the router table (see the photo below). When shopping for an after-market baseplate, look for flatness, a low-friction surface and a removable insert plate or plates that will allow the use of large bits.

An oversized after-market baseplate lets you mount the router in the router table. The baseplate rests on a rabbet the same depth as the thickness of the baseplate, bringing it flush with the table surface.

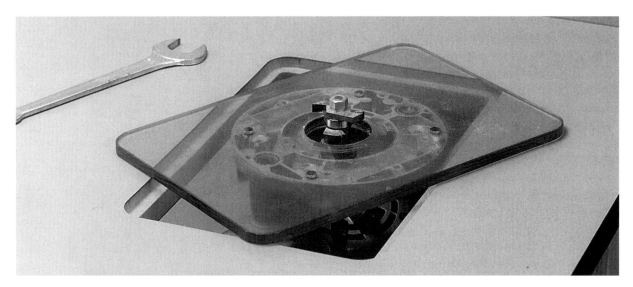

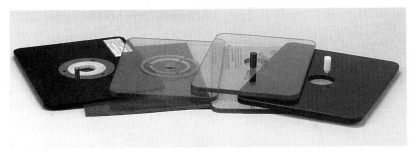

After-market baseplates are made of various materials; some come equipped with a starting pin (see p. 16).

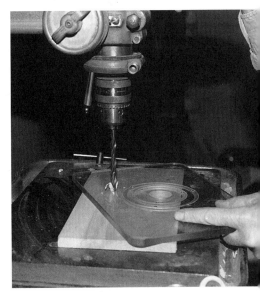

Polycarbonate, phenolic resin and acrylic can all be user fabricated into a baseplate that will fit any router and router-table combination. Here, a piece of polycarbonate is being drilled to receive a mounting screw.

The baseplate material should be easy to work with typical wood-working shop tools. After-market baseplates can be fashioned from various materials (see the photo above), most commonly acrylic, poly-carbonate, phenolic resin, molded plastics and even aluminum. Each has its advantages and disadvantages.

Acrylic (often called Plexiglas, but this is a registered trade name) is cheap and easy to fabricate yourself in the shop. Polycarbonate (Lexan is a common trade name) is the material that helicopter bubbles and shatterproof windows are made of, so it is tough stuff indeed. What is more, it is as easy to work with as acrylic. Acrylic, however, resists sag-ging better and is more consistent in thickness.

Phenolic resin is an excellent baseplate material. It is flat, of constant thickness and resistant to sagging, and it can be drilled and cut easily. Woodhaven offers high-quality baseplates made from ⅜-in. phenolic resin (see Sources of Supply on pp. 114-116). Highland Hardware sells precut ¼-in. thick sheets of phenolic-resin board, along with ⅛-in. thick polycarbonate for insert plates.

You can also get aluminum baseplates. These are soft enough that you can run a bit into them, but they are more difficult to drill, cut or otherwise modify than plastic baseplates. However, of all the base-plate materials, aluminum is the most resistant to sagging.

If you don't want to make your own, various ready-made molded plas-tic baseplates are on the market. Often they have slots instead of holes, so they can mount to many different routers. The quality of these plastic baseplates varies greatly, both among manufacturers and even among batches from the same manufacturer. While some are very good, others are not. I have seen molded baseplates with large ridges where the mold was parted, removable insert rings that did not fit flush and inconsistent thickness. Always inspect baseplates careful-ly before you buy.

Starting pins   Complex shapes are molded by guiding the work with a pilot bearing above or below the cutting edge of the bit (see pp. 69-71). The fence is dispensed with, and the bit protrudes unguarded in the center of the table. To start such work safely, you'll need a starting pin (also called a fulcrum pin). This pin, which is about ¼ in. in diameter, presses into a hole near the bit. In use the work is placed against the pin, then rocked into the spinning cutter until it touches the bearing. From this point on the bearing guides the work. Many baseplates come with a starting pin. If yours doesn't, it is an easy matter to add one. Simply drill a hole slightly to the right and behind the opening for the bit and insert a screw or tapered wood peg.

Auxiliary switches

Many people like to equip their router with a separate switch. This can either be a simple toggle switch located conveniently on the table or a foot switch. I like a simple toggle switch with an outlet that the router plugs into. Reaching under the table and blindly groping for the switch is awkward and risky, and on helical adjusting routers the switch moves each time it is adjusted. A conveniently mounted switch allows easy starting and stopping, especially in an emergency. Being able to unplug the router at the table, rather than having to walk to the wall plug, is also a great convenience.

For some types of work a foot switch (see the photo below) is handy. While some foot switches have the actual switch buried in the foot pedal, others operate pneumatically—you step on a rubber bulb that actuates a relay. The best switches are covered so that they cannot be inadvertently tripped, either by accidentally stepping on them or through something falling on them.

What type of switch you should buy depends largely on the type of work you do. Foot switches are good for repetitive operations like cutting joints with the Incra Jig or JoinTECH (see pp. 42-44). Toggle

A foot switch is a safe, convenient way to start and stop the router.

switches are better for general milling, such as sticking or coping operations. Whatever switch you get, make sure that it is rated to handle the amperage of your router.

Installing and Changing Router Bits

Installing a router bit is simplicity itself. The first step is to unplug the router, even if you have an auxiliary switch. This often overlooked step prevents the router from accidentally being started should the switch inadvertently be brushed. For helical adjusting routers it is often simpler to remove the motor from the base to change bits, especially if two wrenches are involved.

If the shank of the bit does not slide easily into the collet, check for manufacturing problems, such as insufficient radius at the end of the shank, rough finish grinding or a burr. Other times the problem is a roughened interior on the collet or a scratched shank on the bit, which can be caused by the bit spinning in the collet. These problems can be alleviated, if not eliminated, by breaking the edge on a bench grinder and then buffing the shank, as seen in the photo below.

The bit should not bottom out in the collet, for this could prevent the collet from being fully tightened. If the bit shank bottoms out, pull it back out of the collet about $\frac{1}{16}$ in. before tightening the locking nut. Of equal importance is that the bit shank be inserted to sufficient depth to be gripped securely by the collet. Otherwise, the bit may cock sideways and even spin loose.

If the end of the shank is rough and won't fit into the collet, you can break the edge on a bench grinder and then buff it.

Once the bit is engaged, the collet is tightened. Many people tend to overtighten collets, turning the wrenches with the strength of Hercules. Overtightening won't really hurt anything, but it puts unnecessary strain on the collet and makes bit removal much more difficult. When using an adapter bushing, however, more torque is generally necessary so some extra force should be used.

Eye, Ear and Dust Protection

When using a router table, you should take some general precautions to protect your vision, hearing and respiratory system. These include the use of safety glasses, ear protection, dust masks and respirators.

Safety glasses

A spinning router bit throws chips and fine particles into the air, so eye protection during router work is an absolute must. Never turn on a router if you aren't wearing safety glasses. While simple glasses with shatterproof lenses are adequate, true safety glasses with side shields are far better. Some workers may appreciate the additional protection of a face shield.

Ear protection

The router is a noisy tool, generating well above 100 decibels during typical jobs. Exposure to this level of noise will do permanent damage to your hearing. Therefore I consider hearing protection to be essential. Your options include ear plugs, hearing bands and ear muffs; what you choose depends largely on your needs and your budget.

Ear plugs and inserts   The cheapest type of ear protection is a set of ear plugs. These soft rubber plugs are simply inserted in the ears. Rubber plugs are sold in sizes and must be matched to ear size to be effective. They can be washed in warm water when they get dirty and are more apt to be lost than wear out.

Solid plugs have been largely replaced today by soft sponge-rubber ear inserts. These are small cylinders of soft rubber with a chewing-gum-like quality—you simply roll the insert between your fingers until it forms a cone, then place it in the ear canal, where it expands to close out sound. Ear inserts are good for only a few uses, but are very cheap and easy to carry. I keep several pairs in my toolbox for emergencies. The drawback to soft rubber inserts is that they are not easy to put in and take out of your ears and that they can be somewhat uncomfortable when worn for long periods. Since I frequently have to stop working to use the telephone, I find them impractical.

Hearing bands A hearing band is just a set of ear plugs or ear inserts joined by a plastic bow. The bow may be placed above or behind the head, but works equally well under the chin—whichever is most comfortable. When not in use it snaps around your neck out of the way. Bands are cheap and can be carried easily in a toolbox. Since they can be worn around the neck with comfort you need never be without them and hence are more likely to use them.

Ear muffs Ear muffs are plastic cups filled with foam rubber. A spring band goes over the head and holds them tight against the side of the head, where they cover both ears. They block sound effectively and are quick to put on and take off. The only drawback to ear muffs is that they are somewhat uncomfortable to wear around the neck when not in use.

Dust masks and respirators

When using a router table, it is important to protect yourself from dust. Wood dust can be quite toxic and may even be a carcinogen; dust from tropical woods is especially troublesome. Equipping your router table with a vacuum dust pickup (see p. 53) is well worth the effort. But no matter how good your system is, some dust will get into the air, so some kind of dust mask is essential. The simplest and cheapest is a paper dust mask, like those worn in automotive body shops. Better (and more costly) is a respirator, which works like a military gas mask. Respirators offer good dust protection, but are hot and tiring to wear because you are doing the air pumping with your lungs. They also are a problem for people with beards.

Air helmets Powered air respirators (see the photo at right) provide the ultimate protection for your lungs. These air helmets, as they are commonly called, offer the safety of a full face shield and hard hat with excellent dust protection. They have a motor that pumps filtered air into the helmet, so you don't have to make an effort to breathe; the incoming air creates a positive air pressure inside the shield, which excludes dust and prevents fogging. Some air helmets will filter only dust; others also filter organic vapors from finishing products. Ear muffs can be added to most air helmets. Air helmets are quite expensive (as much as $350), but if you do much woodworking they are well worth the price.

An air helmet will protect your eyes and lungs from chips and dust.

CHAPTER 2
Router-Table Design

A router table is basically a simple piece of equipment—just a smooth, level working surface with a router mounted upside-down underneath, its bit protruding through a hole in the table. To this straightforward setup may be added fences, guards, miter slots and devices for dust and chip extraction as well as a host of jigs and other accessories. Elaborate tables differ from simple ones more in the stand and cabinetry underneath the table than in anything else.

If you want a router table you may either buy one or build one yourself. For some people a store-bought table is the better alternative, for the materials necessary for a high-quality shop-built table are often available only through industrial distribution, sometimes, as with sheet goods, in quantities too large for the project at hand. A store-bought table may also be cheaper in the long run, especially if you consider the time it would take you to build one.

On the other hand, building a router table can be an enjoyable project, and you are likely to get a table that better suits your needs. If you already have a lot of the material you need, it will be much cheaper to build one yourself.

If you build your own router table, you can get exactly what you want.
This router table, designed and built by Dave Hout and Ernie Conover,
incorporates such niceties as a plastic-laminate work surface, a drawer
and a storage cabinet.

Two router tables by Eagle feature a centrally mounted baseplate with starting pin and miter slot (right) and and offset-mounted baseplate (below).

Manufactured router tables vary greatly. Some are commercial versions of what is essentially a shop-built router table (see the photos above). The top is fiberboard covered with plastic laminate. The stand is typically wood or metal legs that raise the table to a working height of 32 in. to 36 in. The fences on manufactured router tables vary greatly, but most employ plastic, aluminum extrusions and/or aluminum castings in their design. Manufactured fences often incorporate a vacuum port for dust and chip pickup—a nice feature.

A second type is the high-end metal router table. These cast-iron or cast-aluminum tables have all the features of a well-built machine—flat tables, fine surface finishes and sophisticated fences. Many of them have a miter slot and various optional accessories. One such table is the cast-aluminum router table by Porta-Nails, shown in the photo below. Delta, Porter-Cable, Woodstock International and Nu-Craft Tools also offer cast-metal router tables. These tables list from about $230 to close to $700, but can often be found for less.

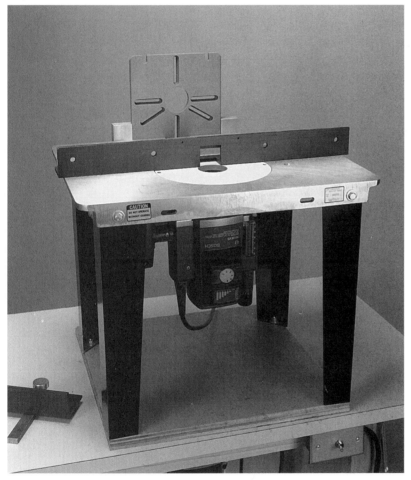

A cast-aluminum router table by Porta-Nails. A second router can be mounted in the right-angle plate at the back of the table to make tenons, dovetails and other precision joinery.

A small, light-duty router table by Porter-Cable (above) and a stamped-metal router table by Sears (right).

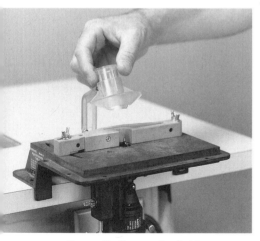

Dremel's tiny router table.

A third type of manufactured router table is mass produced, most often of stamped or injection-molded plastic construction. Such benchtop tables are sold at Sears and at home centers. These small, lightweight tables can be hauled to a job site easily or stored under a bench if shop space is at a premium. They will not, however, handle today's largest routers and bits and are limited to light and medium-duty work. The photos above show two examples of this type of table. There is even a miniature router table for delicate work (see the photo at left).

Finally there are a number of router tables that double as the extension wing of a table saw. Some of these are supplied by the table-saw manufacturer, while others are after-market devices. These tables offer several advantages: They take up little space in the shop, the working height is good, and the table-saw fence can be employed as the router-table fence in some operations. When not in use the router can be left in place with the bit lowered below the table surface so that normal saw operations are not impaired.

Building a Router Table

Building a router table is not a project that requires a high amount of woodworking skill, only basic proficiency. In fact it makes a dandy first project and calls for a variety of procedures that can then be put to use in building kitchen countertops, cabinets and built-ins. What's more, you will end up with a table that is exactly what you want. Even if you decide to buy your router table, reading through this section will let you better evaluate the construction of commercial tables.

A router table can be as simple or as elaborate as you choose to make it. All you really need is a level working surface about 24 in. by 32 in. to 36 in., at a convenient height. I have even made do by clamping a scrap of ½-in. plywood on a workbench, attaching the router base underneath the plywood and using a 2-in. square outrip for a fence. A more usable table would feature a better fence and a plastic-laminate top for a pleasant working surface. On pp. 26-35 are general instructions for building a simple router table with a plastic-laminate top, like the table shown in the drawing below.

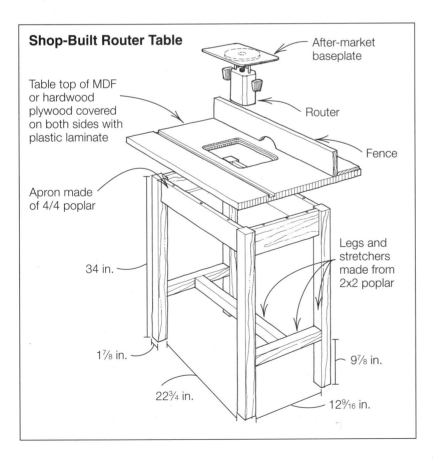

Shop-Built Router Table

After-market baseplate

Table top of MDF or hardwood plywood covered on both sides with plastic laminate

Router

Fence

Apron made of 4/4 poplar

Legs and stretchers made from 2x2 poplar

34 in.

1⅞ in.

9⅞ in.

22¾ in.

12⁹⁄₁₆ in.

Making the table top

The best substrate for the laminate is either medium-density fiber-board (MDF) or high-quality hardwood plywood. If you plan to mill a miter slot in your table (see p. 45) you will need 1-in. thick MDF. If you are not going to include a slot, then ¾-in. MDF will do. High-quality plywood makes a much stronger table than MDF. The best plywood for the job is ¾-in. Baltic birch or apple ply, but lesser grades, which are more widely available at local lumberyards, are also acceptable.

MDF and Baltic birch plywood are often sold only by industrial ply-wood suppliers. Such establishments will often not sell to a private individual. Your local lumberyard may have to order the material for you. You might also try to find a local cabinet shop willing to sell and/or order these materials for you. Some national home-center chains now stock MDF or can get it for you.

Cutting sheet goods   Cutting large sheets of plywood or MDF (especially 1-in. thick MDF) can present some problems because of weight and size. Handling sheet goods is a two-person job. Compounding the problem, most table saws do not have large enough tables to handle 4x8 sheet goods safely, even with two people. One solution is to have the sheet cut for you at the lumberyard on a special saw designed for this purpose, but if you are using Baltic birch plywood or MDF, that may not be an option, since the industrial suppliers that carry these materials seldom offer this service.

My solution is simple: I lay the sheet down on sawhorses and handsaw a piece slightly larger (about 1 in.) than I need. Some may prefer to use a portable circular saw for this job and that is fine, but I find the hand-saw fast and very safe. I lay out the cuts and have a helper support the piece I am cutting free. Yes, I waste a little material this way, but it is far safer than trying to do the job on a small table saw. After the piece is cut to rough size, it can safely be trimmed to its finished dimensions on the table saw. For this 24-in. by 34-in. table top, the best use of materials is to handsaw 25 in. off of the 8-ft. dimension of the sheet. The 48-in. width gives you more than enough material.

Selecting the laminate

For your router table, a thick grade of high-pressure laminate intended for horizontal applications will work best (see the sidebar on the facing page). Plastic laminate is sold in a variety of surface furnishes, and for a router table, a non-glaring, matte surface finish is the best choice. Not only will a matte finish be easier on the eyes, it will also show scratches and wear less. Leftover or scrounged laminate can also be used, of course, and in that case the surface finish really does not matter very much.

Avoid low-pressure laminates that are pre-laminated to high-density fiberboard. This material, called melamine face chipboard (MFC) may seem like a good idea for a router table, but the surface won't be as durable as high-pressure laminate. (Some lower-quality commercial router tables are made from MFC.) If in doubt, you can check the laminate thickness by looking at the hole in the table for the insert plate.

Applying plastic laminate

Once the MDF or plywood table top has been cut to size, you can begin laminating. Plan on covering both sides of the substrate with plastic laminate to exclude moisture and to give the panel more stability. A surface covered on both sides will stay flat in spite of seasonal changes in temperature and humidity. It is all right to use several pieces on the bottom, for a seam or two will not matter. The edges of the substrate

High-Pressure Laminate

Plastic laminate is often referred to as Formica but this name is a registered trademark of the Formica Corporation of Cincinnati, Ohio. The company was founded at the turn of the century when a young Westinghouse chemist, Dan O'Connor, invented the product. Plastic laminate is composed of multiple layers of Kraft paper impregnated with phenolic resin. This sandwich is then covered with a layer of colored (often patterned as well) Kraft paper that is coated with melamine plastic. The entire process is done under immense pressure — in excess of 800 pounds per square inch — to qualify as high-pressure laminate. The original intent for the product was to replace expensive and hard-to-find mica as an electrical insulator — hence the name "formica."

The real market for the product, covering countertops, was found in the late 1930s. Everybody knows just how durable such countertops are, and that is why plastic laminate makes a wonderful surface for a router table. Other companies such as Nevamar, Wilsonart, Lamin-Art and Melamite all make high-pressure laminate that are excellent for a router table.

Because of its original use, standards for plastic laminate are set by the National Electrical Manufacturers Association (NEMA). For router tables we want a NEMA GP-50 grade plastic laminate (Formica Corporation grade 10). This is a rather thick grade of laminate intended for horizontal applications such as countertops. Avoid thinner grades, which are variously called "vertical" or "post forming" grades. Every scratch in the substrate or lump in the glue will "telegraph" through thinner grades, leaving an uneven surface on your router table.

should receive some sort of treatment as well; the possibilities include edge banding with laminate or veneer tape and gluing thin strips of wood to the edge.

Plastic laminate is sold in various lengths and widths, A common one, and a good size for this table top, is 36 in. by 72 in., since we can take the 34-in. dimension out of the width of the sheet. Cutting the laminate to size can be difficult because of the large size of the sheet and the thin, flexible nature of the material. It can be cut on the table saw, but it is thin enough to slip right under the fence of most saws. One solution to the problem is to cut a shallow saw kerf about $\frac{1}{16}$ in. from the bottom of an auxiliary fence and clamp it to the saw, then run the edge of the laminate in the kerf.

If you are working alone, you can simply lay the sheet face down on the floor and mark it for cutting 1 in. oversize. Place a scrap board between the laminate and the floor at the marked area and make four or five passes with a utility knife, applying heavy pressure. When the piece is almost cut through, you can simply bend the panel and it will snap on the line.

Plastic laminate is glued to the substrate using contact cement, and a few precautions are in order. When working with MDF, plastic laminate and contact cement, eye and organic-vapor respiratory protection are mandatory. Also, some cements are explosive, so they should be used with plenty of ventilation and away from sparks or flames. There are safer water-based adhesives, such as Weldwood Poly Acrylic Contact Cement, which is what I used for the table I built for this book, since my shop is heated with a woodstove and I built the table in winter.

The adhesive can be applied with a brush or a roller (I usually buy cheap disposable ones). Apply adhesive to both the back of the laminate and the substrate and let them dry for the amount of time specified in the directions, generally about 20 minutes. Then place the laminate on the substrate (you can't adjust its position once the two touch, so be sure that you put it exactly where you want to) and press it in place. To avoid trapping air bubbles, press the laminate from the center out to the edges. A good way to do this is to place four to six dowels on the glue-covered substrate and then place the glue-covered laminate on top of the dowels, as shown in the drawing on the facing page. When the laminate is aligned as you want it, pull out the center dowel and press down the laminate. Continue in this manner, working out to the edges of the panel.

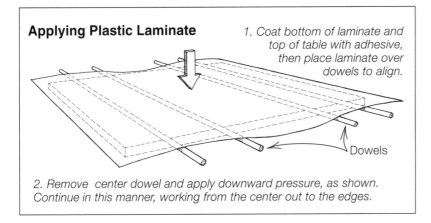

Applying Plastic Laminate

1. Coat bottom of laminate and top of table with adhesive, then place laminate over dowels to align.

Dowels

2. Remove center dowel and apply downward pressure, as shown. Continue in this manner, working from the center out to the edges.

The assembly should be rolled with enough pressure to ensure a good bond between the laminate and the substrate. Special rollers are sold for this purpose, but I have also used a kitchen rolling pin with good results. When you are done, you should have a 24-in. by 34-in. panel, with laminate overhanging about ½ in. on all edges. The overhanging laminate can be trimmed with a hand-held router equipped with a laminate flush-trim bit. Adjust the router until the bit's guide bearing rides along the substrate, and with the assembly clamped to your workbench, work counterclockwise around the assembly until all the edges are trimmed.

Supporting the table

The router table shown in the drawing on p. 25 has simple legs, which I built from 2x2 poplar. I used machine-cut mortise-and-tenon joints in the aprons and stretchers. The top is screwed in place with drywall screws. The top's generous overhang beyond the base make it easy to clamp featherboards and fences to the table. You might want to build a variation of this design on your own table by adding storage compartments underneath.

Installing the router

Although the router may be attached directly to the underside of the top with screws, this is not a good option. A more versatile means of attachment is through an after-market baseplate, or table insert, which replaces the standard router baseplate and sits on a rabbet around a rectangular cutout in the router table. The rabbet is exactly the height of the baseplate so that the insert will come flush with the table top. Although it takes a little time to attach the table insert to the router and to cut the matching hole in the table top, you'll find it time well spent when you do.

The simplest way to cut the rabbeted hole is with a hand-held router. This hole may be located either in the center of the table or offset to one side (see the photos on p. 22). With a centrally located hole (which I prefer), there is plenty of room behind the bit for the fence and enough room in front of the bit for the widest of work plus hold-downs. A miter slot can be milled the length of the table in front of the bit. If the slot is inconvenient for a particular job, the table can be turned around.

Offsetting the hole to one end of the table lets you work across the table rather then along the length of it. This is desirable for two reasons. First, relatively short infeed and outfeed surfaces facilitate sticking operations with long work that is bowed. Second, the offset placement better facilitates use of commercial positioning systems, such as the Incra Jig or the JoinTECH system (see pp. 42-44), since both of these systems require a lot of table in back of the fence for attachment. An offset router placement allows this with no modification to the table. These systems can, however, be used with a centrally mounted router by adding an extra piece of plywood or MDF on the back of the router table.

I favor the central hole location even for use with the Incra Pro or the JoinTECH. Most of the time I keep the miter slot to the back of the table, where it's out of the way.

Certain operations, such as running molding (see p. 89), go better if the hole in the table insert is as small as possible. For this reason I favor inserts that have removable rings (see the photo below), so that the

A table insert with removable rings allows you to tailor the size of the opening to the diameter of the bit being used. This feature makes for the trouble-free feeding of stock past the bit and for more efficient dust evacuation, which results in cleaner, cooler cuts.

size of the opening can be increased or decreased as needed. If the opening is considerably larger than the bit, stock can be forced down into the opening by the featherboards, causing a jam. Additionally dust evacuation is not nearly as efficient, due to the increased ingress of air from below the table. Finally debris can fall through the opening, causing the motor to overheat.

Cutting the rabbeted hole   Routing the rabbeted hole for a replaceable table insert is a three-step operation. You use the table insert to make a template for cutting the hole (Step 1), then you cut the hole in the table top (Step 2) and finally you cut the rabbet (Step 3). The hole in the table is cut with a hand-held plunge router guided by a guide bushing that follows the edge of a template made from the table insert (for an explanation of template routing, see p. 73). The rabbet into which the table insert sets is then cut with the router guided by a pilot bearing. Since bits can vary considerably in diameter, it is always wise to make test cuts on scrap stock.

To do this work I used a plunge router, a piece of MDF $\frac{1}{2}$ in. thick for the template, a roll of double-sided tape, a $\frac{1}{4}$-in. dia. spiral-fluted straight bit, a piloted rabbeting bit, and $\frac{1}{2}$-in. and $1\frac{1}{2}$-in. guide bushings. The drawing on p. 32 summarizes the process, which is also shown in the photo-essay on pp. 34-35. You can also use other combinations of bit sizes and guide-bushing diameters, but you will have to work through the offset calculations yourself. (For a discussion of offset, see p. 77.)

With a hand-held router, it is important to realize that the feed direction is the opposite of the feed direction for router-table work (see pp. 80-81), since the router is now right side up and the cutter is turning clockwise as viewed from above. Therefore you rout counterclockwise around the outside of a template and clockwise around the inside of a template.

Routing a Rabbeted Hole for the Table Insert

Step 1: Cutting the Template

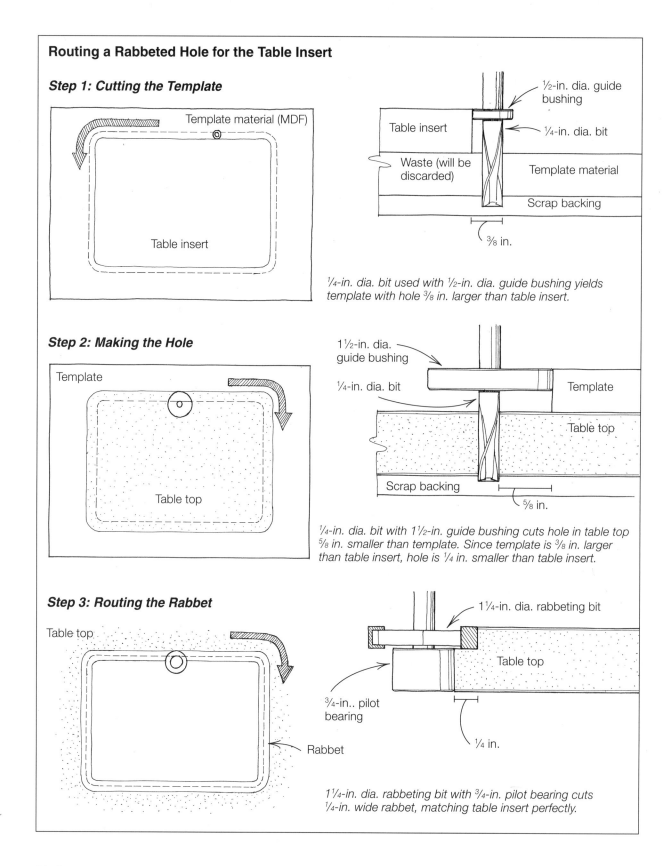

Template material (MDF)

Table insert

½-in. dia. guide bushing

Table insert

¼-in. dia. bit

Waste (will be discarded)

Template material

Scrap backing

⅜ in.

¼-in. dia. bit used with ½-in. dia. guide bushing yields template with hole ⅜ in. larger than table insert.

Step 2: Making the Hole

Template

Table top

1½-in. dia. guide bushing

¼-in. dia. bit

Template

Table top

Scrap backing

⅝ in.

¼-in. dia. bit with 1½-in. guide bushing cuts hole in table top ⅝ in. smaller than template. Since template is ⅜ in. larger than table insert, hole is ¼ in. smaller than table insert.

Step 3: Routing the Rabbet

Table top

Rabbet

1¼-in. dia. rabbeting bit

Table top

¾-in.. pilot bearing

¼ in.

1¼-in. dia. rabbeting bit with ¾-in. pilot bearing cuts ¼-in. wide rabbet, matching table insert perfectly.

Begin by making a template for cutting the hole. Tape the baseplate to the template material (see photo 1 on p. 34), using the double-sided tape. Also tape a scrap piece of material to the underside of the template material to support the loose piece as it is cut free. Otherwise the baseplate will move as the cut is completed and the template will not be perfect.

Now using the $\frac{1}{4}$-in. spiral-fluted bit and the $\frac{1}{2}$-in. guide bushing, rout around the table insert in a counterclockwise direction (photo 2). Do not try this in one pass; use the click stops on the plunge router to lower the bit about $\frac{1}{4}$ in. at a time. It will take two or three cuts to break through, depending on the thickness of the MDF template material. Because of the bit/bushing offset, the opening in the finished template will be $\frac{3}{8}$ in. bigger than the table insert (photo 3).

To cut the hole, tape the template to the table top, again taping a piece of scrap to the underside to support the loose piece as it is cut free. Switch to the $1\frac{1}{2}$-in. guide bushing and cut the rough opening (see photo 4 on p. 35), making two or three passes in a clockwise direction until full depth is reached. Because of the bit/bushing offset, the hole you cut in the table top will be $\frac{5}{8}$ in. smaller than the template, and since the template is $\frac{3}{8}$ in. larger than the table insert, the hole will be $\frac{1}{4}$ in. smaller than the table insert.

To cut the rabbet, remove the guide bushing and use a piloted rabbeting bit with a $\frac{3}{4}$-in. pilot bearing. Rout clockwise around the inside of the template, into the direction the bit is spinning (photo 5). As you did when routing the template in Step 1, make shallow cuts and repeated passes to full depth, which should match the thickness of the table insert. Check frequently. If you have cut too deep, glue in shims and recut.

Do not be dismayed if the finished opening (photo 6) is not a perfect fit, for bits and guide bushings vary considerably. Also, the bushing may not always be perfectly concentric with the collet. If the opening is too small, simply trim the table insert down a bit with a hand plane or a sander. If the opening is too large, shim it with tape or a thin strip of wood.

Routing a rabbeted hole

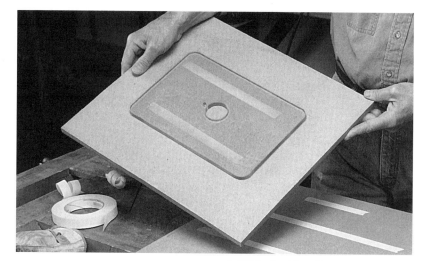

1. With double-sided tape, attach the table insert to the template material. Scrap should also be taped to the underside of the template material to support the loose piece as it is cut free.

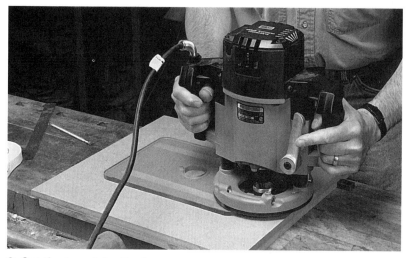

2. Cut the template. Rout counterclockwise around the table insert, using a ¼-in. spiral-fluted straight bit and a ½-in. guide bushing. Make two to three passes, lowering the bit each time.

3. Lift the finished template free.

4. Cut the hole. With the template taped to the router table top and a piece of scrap taped underneath the workpiece for support, rout clockwise around the inside of the template, using the ¼-in. bit and a 1½-in. guide bushing.

5. Cut the rabbet, routing clockwise around the hole, using a piloted rabbeting bit with a ¾-in. pilot bearing.

6. The table insert sits in the finished rabbeted opening flush with the surface of the table top.

Fences

The fence serves several purposes. It guides the work past the cutter, provides vacuum pickup for dust and chip evacuation and, to varying degrees, guards the cutter. The fence is in essence no more than a large right-angle block that is attached to the router table, either permanently or with clamps. While most commercial tables come with a fence (on some it is an option), a fence can easily be shop built. In fact I think the shop built is superior in most cases.

Commercial fences are usually built from structural foam, plastic or an aluminum extrusion or aluminum castings. A must for aluminum extrusions is anodizing, a plating process that puts a protective coating on the aluminum. Without anodizing the aluminum will blacken everything it touches. The coating can be clear or colored.

Some fences are entirely aluminum while others face the extrusion with wood, and the latter is definitely a better option. A fence is virtually useless unless the working surface is at exactly 90° to the table, but many stock aluminum extrusions are not perfectly square. If the

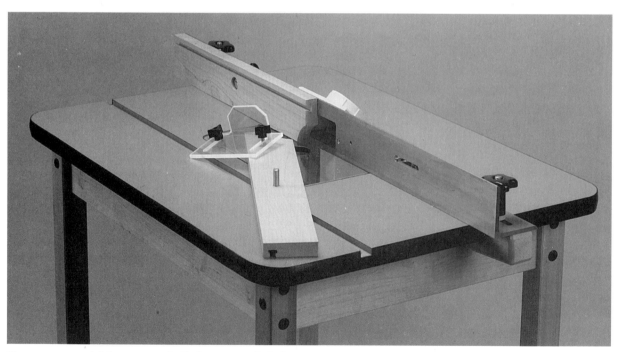

Many commercial fences are built from extruded aluminum.

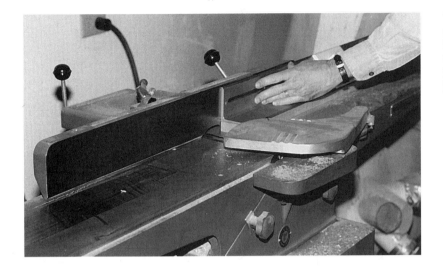

fence is faced with wood, the entire assembly can be run through a jointer and made square. To square a fence, set the jointer to a light cut of $\frac{1}{16}$ in. or less, place the wood face of the fence down on the jointer table and run it through while holding the aluminum web firmly against the jointer fence, as shown in the photo above. (Before you begin, make sure that that all the hardware is countersunk more than $\frac{1}{16}$ in. below the surface of the wood so that you do not hit any metal with your jointer cutter head.) The fence may also be jointed with a hand plane.

Many commercial fences have a circular or rectangular opening in the fence for the router bit. For good milling it is important to have the fence as close as possible to the bit. When the fence supports the work as it is being cut by the bit, splintering ahead of the cutter is greatly reduced and a better finish is achieved. Dust and chip extraction is also greatly improved.

Split fences (see the photo on p. 38) have separate pieces of wood attached to the infeed and outfeed halves of the aluminum extrusion. These pieces can be slid laterally along the extrusion to adjust the size of the opening around the bit—this is a desirable feature in a router-table fence.

Commercial fences are attached to the table in a variety of ways. In one common system, studs with plastic knobs through slots in the aluminum extrusion mate with threaded metal inserts in the router table. Systems like this have a limited amount of adjustment. I prefer to lock down a fence with C-clamps or quick-action clamps, which allow you

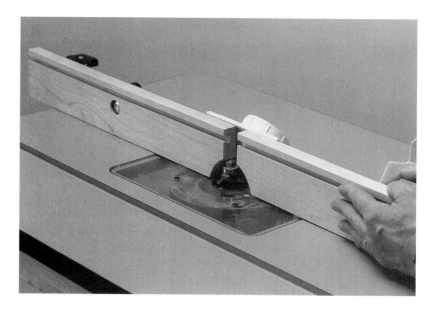

to orient the fence in any position at all and still lock it rock solid. Quick-action clamps can be operated with one hand, a definite plus, so you can use your other hand to hold the fence in place while you clamp it. One never has enough hands when setting a fence.

Shop-built fences

Making a fence takes so little time that you can make several for different applications. I usually build fences from poplar but any scrap wood (including plywood or MDF) will do if it is straight. The height of the fence should be at least 3 in., but with a higher fence it's easier to clamp on featherboards, vacuum ports and guards over the cutter. A height of 4 in. is good; a height of 5 in. or 6 in. is nice for some work, such as raising panels with a vertical panel-raising bit (see p. 110).

A typical shop-made fence is shown in the drawing on the facing page. The two parts of the fence may be glued together. If you have a biscuit joiner or a doweling jig, it will be easier to register the two pieces precisely to one another.

Most general routing can be handled with three shop-made fences with progressively bigger openings—small, medium and large. Certain operations, such as running molding, require a fence with an opening that matches the profile of the bit—a zero-clearance fence. With a zero-clearance fence, chipping and splintering along the grain in front of the cutter are greatly reduced, and dust pickup is improved. Commercial fences that are or can be faced with wood can be converted to zero-clearance fences, as can any shop-made wood fence. On split fences where the two halves can slide left and right, obtaining zero clearance is easy, although new wood parts may have to be made. Just set the fence normally, turn on the router, loosen the fence parts a little and slide them until the bit just mills its profile in the fence opening. Depending on the demands of the operation, this may be done to the infeed side only or to both sides of the fence.

Making a zero-clearance fence   It is easy to incorporate zero clearance into a shop-built fence like the one in the drawing below. I do this by drawing out the profile of the bit on the upright section of the fence before gluing the halves together (see photo 1 on p. 40). With a scroll-saw or bandsaw, I then cut inside the lines where the cutting edge is and outside the lines where the bearing and shaft are, then assemble the fence (photo 2). When the glue is dry, line up the fence next to the cutter, clamp one edge of the fence to the table (see photo 3 on p. 41), turn on the router and slowly pivot the fence opening over the bit (photo 4). The result is an opening that matches the profile of the bit.

A Shop-Built Fence

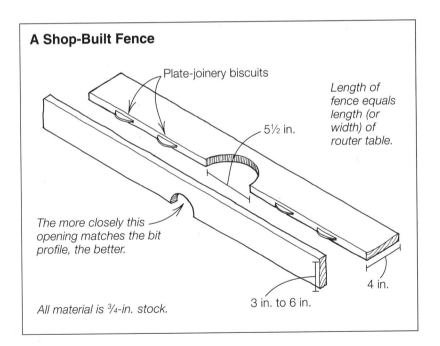

Plate-joinery biscuits

5½ in.

Length of fence equals length (or width) of router table.

The more closely this opening matches the bit profile, the better.

4 in.

3 in. to 6 in.

All material is ¾-in. stock.

Making a zero-clearance fence

1. Lay out the bit opening on the upright section of the fence, and a semicircular opening on the flat section. (above)

2. After sawing a notch in the fence and cutting out the semicircular opening, glue the fence parts together. (at left)

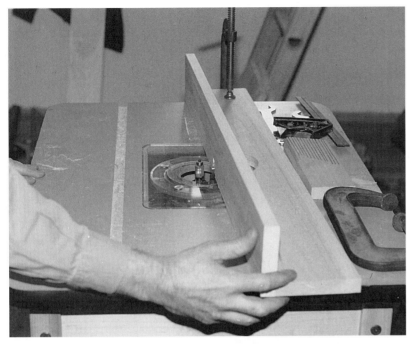

3. With the fence aligned and clamped down on one edge, pivot the bit opening through the cutter. (above)

4. The bit cuts its profile in the upright part of the fence. (at right)

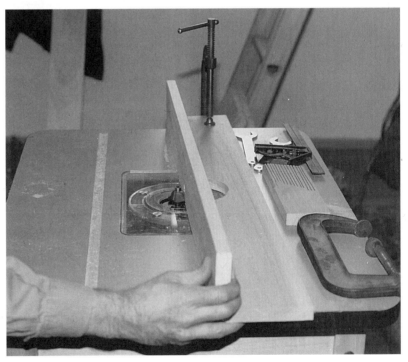

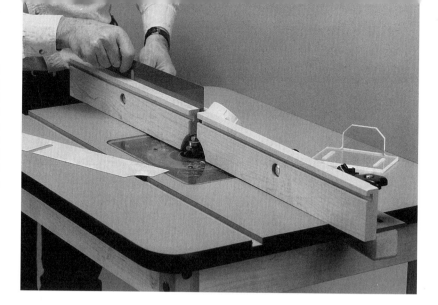

The outfeed half of most commercial fences can be offset in some way to support a workpiece when the entire face of the work has been routed. Here a shim is inserted between the wood part of the fence and the aluminum extrusion.

For most router-table operations the fence is clamped in place over or to one side of the bit, which spins counterclockwise. The workpiece is held against the fence and moved past the bit from the infeed side of the table. As the bit makes its cut along the face of the workpiece, the table surface and the fence support the workpiece and keep it moving in a straight line.

If you are routing the entire face of the work, the outfeed side of the fence needs to be shimmed a bit proud of the infeed side by the amount removed by the cutter so the fence will support the work after it has been milled. I glue thin cardboard and/or 1/16-in. plywood to the outfeed half of the fence using photo-mount adhesive. Better commercial router tables have mechanisms for shimming or offsetting the outfeed half of the fence, as shown in the photo above.

Once a fence is clamped to the table (I like to use C-clamps), small adjustments in position can be made with a wood mallet by loosening one clamp and tapping the fence at that end, then retightening the clamp. Unlike fences on bandsaws and table saws, router-table fences don't have to be square to the cutter. Adjusting a fence to a router bit is a radial problem, so pivoting the fence from one end works fine.

Commercial positioning systems

Many users elect to equip their router table with a precision fence-positioning system. Two such systems currently on the market are the Incra Jig and the JoinTECH (see the photos on the facing page). The advantage of these systems is their ability to put a router-table fence exactly where you want it in an instant. Once aligned, the fence always stays parallel to the miter slot, if there is one.

The original Incra Jig and its current incarnation, the Incra Pro, use two plastic racks that slide together like a miniature extension ladder to position the extruded aluminum fence in $\frac{1}{32}$-in. increments. Raising a toggle allows the two halves of the extrusion to be moved easily. Flipping the toggle to either side locks the two racks firmly together at the desired measurement. A sliding hairline allows precise reading of an excellent ruler in the top extrusion. The ruler is graduated in very readable thirty-seconds to match the rack distances. Numerous accessories that can be added to the system, such as the Incra Mike, allow additional fine adjustment down to .001 in. between the $\frac{1}{32}$-in. increments of the plastic racks.

The JoinTECH is also built of aluminum extrusions, and achieves the same results as the Incra Pro by different means. The basis of the system is the IPM (Incremental Positioning Machine), a heavy, chrome-

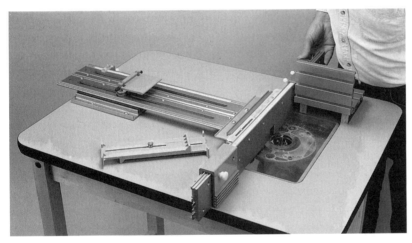

The Incra Pro fence-adjusting system uses plastic racks to move the fence in $\frac{1}{32}$-in. increments.

The JoinTECH adjusts fence position through a lead-screw mechanism.

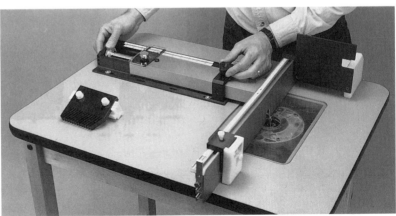

plated, 32-threads-per-inch lead screw. The jig is controlled by turning a large knurled knob that has 16 click stops per revolution, which works out to about .002 in. per click. The lead screw runs in a set of pivots in the base extrusions and engages a half-nut in the other extrusion. Pushing a large chrome button disengages the half-nut and allows quick coarse adjustments anywhere within the range of the IPM. With the half-nut disengaged, the two halves of the IPM run smoothly on nylon rollers.

Both companies offer an aluminum-extrusion fence and numerous further accessories, such as a fence-guided miter gauge and stops for serial production. Neither fence can be faced with wood (a serious drawback, but you can attach a shop-made fence to the JoinTECH IPM).

These systems are quite popular in spite of their cost—about $175 for the Incra Pro and $200 for the JoinTECH. Many people who buy these systems are seduced by the current trend of what I call three-significant-place woodworking. Striving for accuracy beyond sixty-fourths is overkill in a dimensionally unstable medium like wood. Fine adjustments are nice, but don't get carried away. An additional lure of Incra and JoinTECH is the nifty joinery that can be made with them, most notably a dovetail within a dovetail—a real crowd grabber when the technique is demonstrated at woodworking shows.

Miter Slots and Miter Gauges

The miter slot is a groove in the router table top that runs parallel to the fence, into which fits a standard miter gauge (like the one in your table saw). There are also fence-guided miter gauges (see below), and opinions vary as to which is better. Some people find a miter slot indispensable, while others think that the slot weakens the table and makes it more likely to warp.

I think that fence-guided miter gauges are, for the most part, better, but that the miter slot comes in handy at times, especially for jigs that can run in it. A sturdy table with a good stand is unlikely to warp, and even if it did, it could be pulled back straight by screwing wood or metal cleats to the underside of the table.

On tables with centrally mounted routers, the miter slot can be turned to the back when it is not needed. With offset mounting, the miter slot can be filled with a strip of wood to bring the surface flush with the rest of the table when not in use.

Milling the miter slot

The standard miter slot is ¾ in. wide by ⅜ in. deep and can best be milled with a hand-held router. The location of the miter slot will depend somewhat on the size of your miter gauge (I use the one from my table saw). The slot should be far enough from the router that the miter gauge will clear the biggest bits you plan to run by about ½ in. On my table, I allowed for 3-in. bits to be on the safe side. Once you have decided on a location, use a builder's square to mark the sides of the slot with pencil lines (Step 1 in the drawing at right). Now install the table insert in the table, set the largest bit you plan to run (or a top-view drawing of it if you don't own it yet) in the insert and set the miter gauge between the pencil lines (Step 2). If the clearances are right, simply install a ¾-in. bit in your hand-held router and use a scrap length of wood that has been jointed straight as a guide. The edge of the router baseplate will bear against this straightedge, so you'll have to offset it from the intended location of the near edge of the slot by half the diameter of the baseplate minus half the diameter of the bit. Always place the straightedge to the left side of the router so that cutter rotation will naturally hold the router against the straightedge.

When the straightedge is at the proper offset from the left edge of the slot location, mill the slot with the hand-held router (Step 3). Do this job in two or three passes. It's a good idea to make a test cut first in scrap material to check the fit of the miter gauge. If it's too snug, you can move the straightedge to the left just a tad and make a second pass, but since only one side of the bit will be working, you have to exercise extra caution to hold the router against the straightedge.

The miter gauge should have a good sliding fit, but not rattle side to side. Woodhaven and Eagle now offer aluminum extrusions that can be mounted in an oversized slot; these make the milling job less critical and present a low-wear surface for the miter gauge to run in. Woodhaven's extrusion, designed by Mark Duginske, has the added feature that the running fit of the miter gauge may be adjusted at any time. Tightening the mounting screws at the bottom of the extrusion pinches the sides tighter to take up wear. It is a good idea.

Milling a miter slot is so simple that I seldom incorporate one into a table until I need it. Once it's there, I keep the slot to the back of the table most of the time and turn the entire table around when I do need to use it.

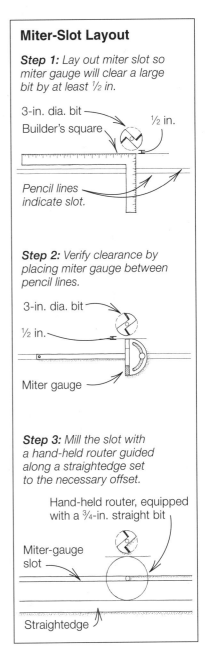

Miter-Slot Layout

Step 1: Lay out miter slot so miter gauge will clear a large bit by at least ½ in.

3-in. dia. bit
½ in.
Builder's square

Pencil lines indicate slot.

Step 2: Verify clearance by placing miter gauge between pencil lines.

3-in. dia. bit
½ in.
Miter gauge

Step 3: Mill the slot with a hand-held router guided along a straightedge set to the necessary offset.

Hand-held router, equipped with a ¾-in. straight bit

Miter-gauge slot

Straightedge

Miter gauges

There are several choices when it comes to miter gauges for the router table. They include the traditional metal slot-guided miter gauge, the wraparound design, the quick and dirty miter gauge and a bushing-guided miter-gauge.

Slot-guided miter gauge   A conventional miter gauge, like the one in a table saw, works well for running shop-made or commercial jigs. If you are making end-grain cuts, however, you will have to back up the work either by placing a waste piece behind it or by screwing or taping a waste strip to the miter gauge and running it through the cutter first. Both alternatives are unwieldy and time-consuming—for this operation, a fence-guided miter gauge works better.

A traditional commercial miter gauge can be used with a router table, but end-grain cuts must be backed up with a scrap piece.

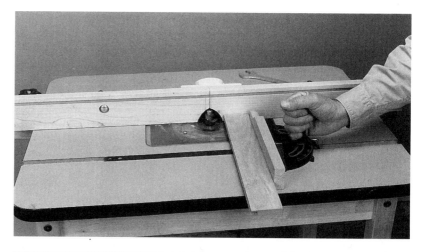

A wraparound miter gauge guides off the fence itself, so it cannot get out of alignment. It is quick to get into operation but will not pass under featherboards and guards.

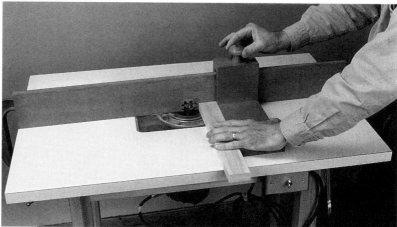

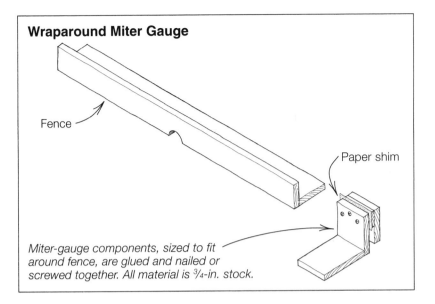

Wraparound Miter Gauge

Fence

Paper shim

Miter-gauge components, sized to fit around fence, are glued and nailed or screwed together. All material is ¾-in. stock.

Wraparound miter gauge Many workers make a simple wraparound miter gauge that wraps up and around the fence as shown in the bottom photo on the facing page, so the miter gauge stays snug against the fence and square to it. The wraparound miter gauge is particularly useful when coping narrow workpieces, such as rails for a cabinet door. It allows the operator to concentrate on process and not have the additional worry of keeping the miter gauge, as well as the workpiece, in the proper relationship to the fence. It is also good for beginners and students because there is less to go wrong.

One design for a wraparound miter gauge is shown in the drawing above. To eliminate seasonal expansion and contraction (binding in the hot, humid summer and a loose fit in the cold, dry winter), make the wraparound gauge from the same material, in the same grain orientation, as the fence. Adding a paper shim to the assembly during glue-up will make for a perfect fit over the fence.

Incra Pro and JoinTECH (see Sources of Supply on pp. 114-116) offer commercial versions of the wraparound miter gauge. Because they are made of plastic and run on an aluminum fence, seasonal movement is not a problem. The JoinTECH version is even adjustable as to fit. However, both miter gauges are small and suited only to small-scale work with bits that can fit within either system's small fence openings.

The quick and dirty miter gauge is cheap and easy to make and has the advantage of passing under featherboards and commercial guards.

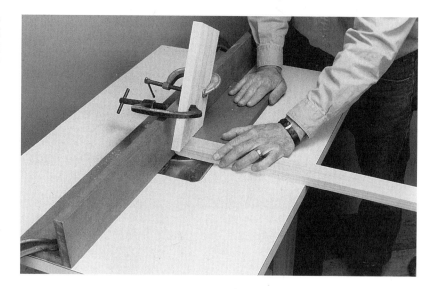

Quick and dirty miter gauge   The quick and dirty miter gauge is nothing more than a squared-off scrap block that slides along the fence (see the photo above), and for ease of construction and cheapness of manufacture it wins hands down. All cuts are backed up well and hands can be clear of the bit. The block can be turned end for end and used for another pass, after which it can be trimmed shorter or discarded. Its only failing is that it is not as easy to keep snug to the fence as the wraparound design. The block should be long enough and wide enough to keep your hands well clear of the cutter. I generally start with the longest piece I can find so that I can cut the ends back once or twice for additional uses.

For my own work I use the quick and dirty miter gauge most of the time. It is the quickest to make, works well and can pass under featherboards and commercial guards .

Bushing-guided miter gauge   The bushing-guided miter gauge is splendid for cutting small dadoes, sliding dovetails and other such work on narrow stock (less than 6 in. wide). It is useful for wasting the cheeks of a tenon, the shoulders of which were first cut on a table saw. It is also good as the basis of other router jigs, such as for cutting finger joints (see pp. 101-102). I use it the most for cutting dadoes for drawer dividers. It's not so good for most end-grain cuts because it's hard to guard the bit when using it. For safety reasons, I never use this carriage with bits larger than ¾-in. diameter.

Plans for this miter gauge are shown in the drawing below. Construction is not fussy, but the base should be made of ½-in. plywood, the slot should be milled to an exact fit with the guide bushing, and the middle solid-wood crosspiece must be at 90° to the slot. Any size guide bushing will work with this gauge, and the larger the bushing, the larger the bit you'll be able to use. A ¾-in. bushing is good because you can use a ½-in. bit.

To use the gauge, just put the workpiece against the middle crosspiece, adjust the bit height and slide the gauge across the table. As long as the workpiece remains stationary relative to the gauge, the cut will be straight, since the gauge is radially guided by the guide bushing.

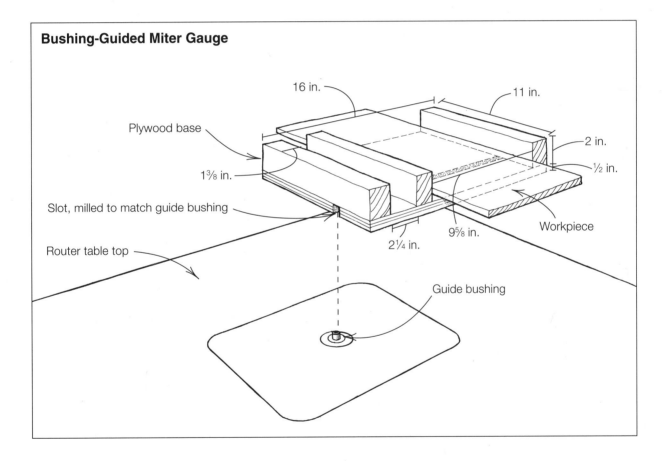

Bushing-Guided Miter Gauge

16 in.

11 in.

Plywood base

2 in.

½ in.

1⅜ in.

Slot, milled to match guide bushing

9⅝ in.

Workpiece

Router table top

2¼ in.

Guide bushing

Safety Guards and Featherboards

To work safely on a router table you must address two main problems: keeping your hands away from the bit and controlling the path of the workpiece as it moves past the cutter. There are commercial guards, both built-in and after market, that shield the bit. You can also devise your own guards for specific applications, along the lines of my designs detailed below. There are also commercial wheeled hold-down devices that can be used to guide the workpiece past the bit (see the top drawing on p. 81). A much simpler item that will accomplish the same purpose is the featherboard, which you can make in your own shop at virtually no cost.

Halo guards

Most commercial router tables come with some sort of guard, often a right-angled piece of red or orange transparent plastic, which attaches to or protrudes from the fence and can be positioned over the bit (see the photo at left). While these guards won't absolutely keep you from inadvertently touching the bit, they have value because they give you a sense of where the bit is. A spinning router bit becomes nearly invisible (especially at the periphery of large bits), and a brightly colored "halo" guard clearly delineates the danger zone. It's a good idea to use such a guard even on shop-made fences. Halo guards can be purchased or shop made.

Guard for pilot-bearing work

Some router-table operations are done without the fence in place, for example using a bit equipped with a pilot bearing to mill a curved edge (see p. 109). This can be a very dangerous setup because the bit protrudes unprotected through the center of the table, so some sort of guard is essential. I know of no commercial guard for such work, but fortunately it is a simple matter to make one in the shop.

As shown in the top drawing on the facing page, the guard is made from wood. The top piece forms an umbrella over the bit, and should overhang it generously on all sides and be $1/16$ in. higher than the work. The channel under the guard formed by the two side cleats allows vacuum pickup, something not otherwise possible with an exposed cutter. This guard should take less than 30 minutes to make and can be used with a variety of bits.

In use, the guard is positioned over the cutter and starting pin and clamped to the table. The work must be slid under the overhang to contact the bit and should a kickback occur the overhang will brush your fingers away, keeping them out of the cutter. The hole in the middle lets you see when the edge of the workpiece or template contacts the pilot bearing and when to end the cut.

Most commercial fences come with a red or orange plastic halo guard that alerts you to the danger zone of the whirling router bit.

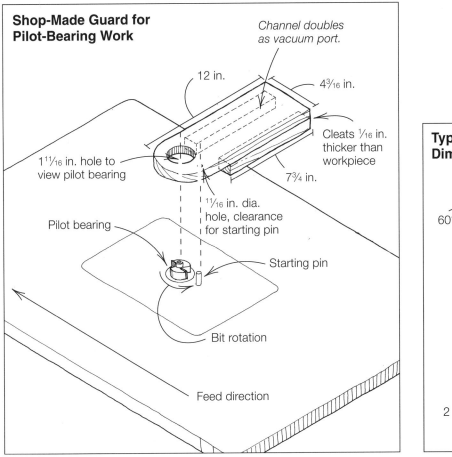

Shop-Made Guard for Pilot-Bearing Work

Channel doubles as vacuum port.

12 in.

4³⁄₁₆ in.

Cleats ¹⁄₁₆ in. thicker than workpiece

1¹¹⁄₁₆ in. hole to view pilot bearing

7¾ in.

¹¹⁄₁₆ in. dia. hole, clearance for starting pin

Pilot bearing

Starting pin

Bit rotation

Feed direction

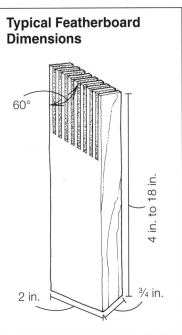

Typical Featherboard Dimensions

60°

4 in. to 18 in.

2 in.

¾ in.

Featherboards

A featherboard is an angled piece of wood with a series of saw kerfs through one end (see the drawing at right). Featherboards perform two functions. On fence-guided cuts, they hold the work down firmly on the table and against the fence, especially around the bit, eliminating or greatly reducing chatter and yielding a much straighter, smoother profile. Even if the operator stops feeding the workpiece midway through the cut, there will be no telltale ledge (if the bit is sharp, there won't even be a burn mark) and the operator can walk to the outfeed side of the table and pull the remaining stock through. Because they are angled, featherboards also prevent reverse feeding of the workpiece and protect the operator in the event of a kickback. Kickback occurs when the work is pushed backwards by the bit. Positioning a featherboard over the cutter often serves the same purpose as a halo guard, and most router-table setups benefit from a featherboard in this position.

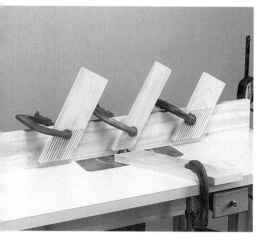

Featherboards hold work down firmly against the fence and the router table for a chatter-free finish. The angled 'feathers' also prevent the work from kicking back at the operator.

Featherboards can easily be made with a backsaw.

Featherboards are easily made in the shop. The drawing on p. 51 gives dimensions I've found useful in my router-table work, but you should feel free to improvise. You can cut the parallel slots using a table saw or a bandsaw. Make the cuts close enough that the fingers are springy. I find that fingers $\frac{1}{16}$ in. to $\frac{1}{8}$ in. wide work well. On the table saw, I cut the 60° angle on one end, then cut the fingers. I start with a piece of stock long enough that I can make the series of parallel cuts without getting my fingers close to the blade, then trim to length later. On the bandsaw, I first trim the end to about 60°, then make a series of parallel cuts. Take care when withdrawing the work after each cut that you don't pull the blade out of the guides and/or off the wheels. If you don't have a table saw or a bandsaw, you can use a backsaw (see the photo above right).

In use, featherboards are clamped to the fence or to the router table top, as shown in the photo above left. Any molding setup needs at least one featherboard and can have as many as necessary hold the work firmly against the table.

Dust and Chip Extraction

Routing creates a lot of dust and debris, so hooking a shop vacuum or a dust collector to your router table makes a lot of sense. Most commercial fences have some provision for dust collection, usually a plastic box section built into the fence just behind the opening for the router bit (see the photo below left) for attaching the hose of an industrial vacuum or dust collector. You can easily fabricate a similar pickup from cardboard or thin plywood and duct-tape it to an opening in a shop-built fence (see the photo below right).

Not all the dust goes up, however; some of it is pulled down through the hole in the table. Keeping the baseplate opening as near the diameter of the bit as possible will limit the amount of debris that falls through. Plates with removable and replaceable rings (see the photo on p. 30) are most helpful here. You might also consider adding some sort of dust pickup underneath the table—either a built-in system or a flexible-hose and duct-tape arrangement. Such a pickup is best placed at the rear underside of the table, just behind the opening. This usually works out to be just below the fence pickup. On exposed-bit operations, strategically placing the vacuum hose is difficult. The shop-built guard for pilot-bearing work described on pp. 50-51, which incorporates dust pickup, is one solution to the problem.

Most commercial fences have provision for hooking up an industrial vacuum or dust collector.

A dust pickup can be fabricated from cardboard and attached to a shop-built fence with duct tape.

Router Bits

Router bits are the business end of the router. We often take these little chunks of metal for granted, but they are the most important factor in getting good results with the router table. Don't economize on bits. That is not to say one must always pick the most expensive bit, but poor bits will always give poor results. Much goes into making a good router bit, and understanding the manufacturing process may increase your appreciation for these mundane but useful objects. Understanding how bits cut will help you keep them sharp.

Bits are commonly manufactured in two grades. Lower-quality bits may be referred to as "home owner" or "DIY" grade; better-quality bits may be referred to as "commercial" or "industrial" grade. Serious workers should try to avoid lower-quality bits for anything but one-time use.

High-Speed-Steel vs. Carbide Bits

With router bits, there are two main choices: high-speed-steel (HSS) bits and carbide bits, and each has its advantages and disadvantages. Either type of bit is widely available through specialty catalogs, machinery and tool dealers, home centers, lumberyards and hardware

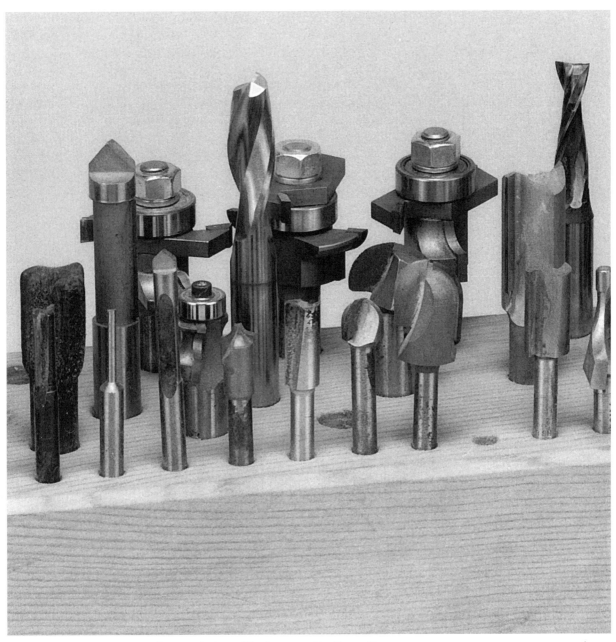

Router bits come in many sizes and sizes. Start your collection with a
few common profiles; acquire more specialized bits as you need them.

stores. However, the bits found in home centers, lumberyards and hardware stores are often DIY grade, but a recent trend is for many of these establishments to stock industrial-quality bits as well.

Most people think HSS bits are not worthy of consideration by a serious craftsperson, but nothing could be farther from the truth. This is because the very cheapest of bits are HSS. Many have bought such bits and been disappointed. HSS bits are made at all quality levels, and while the low-quality home-owner type should be avoided, the high-quality industrial type will give long and faithful service. In fact many furniture manufacturers buy large quantities of HSS bits for production purposes. In addition to being cheaper to buy in the first place, HSS bits cut cleaner because they can be brought to a finer and sharper edge than carbide bits (for information on sharpening, see pp. 61-62). High-speed-steel bits are great for special-purpose jobs that probably will never be repeated. Most spiral-fluted bits (see pp. 65) are high-speed steel.

About 75% of the bits sold are carbide bits. They are very popular because they hold an edge much longer than HSS (although they are more difficult and time-consuming to sharpen). How much longer varies tremendously with the circumstances of use, but estimates vary from a worst case of five to as much as fifty times longer.

Anti-kickback bits

You many want to consider using anti-kickback bits, especially if you are a beginner, since they will afford you an extra measure of safety. Unlike other carbide bits, whose cutting tips extend fairly far from the body, anti-kickback bits have a body almost as large as their cutting diameter. In these bits the flutes are slots in the body instead of large cutouts (see the drawing at left), so the amount of material removed with each pass is limited. In other words, these bits do not dig in deeply as they cut, so the risk of kickback is minimized. They are of some value with the router table when an operator feeds stock into the bit too vigorously, but they are not an absolute assurance against overfeeding accidents. The anti-kickback design was developed some years ago in Germany, but today these bits are made by several of the major manufacturers and readily available in this country.

Anti-kickback vs. conventional design

An anti-kickback bit limits the bite of the cutter at each revolution, so kickback is unlikely.

A standard bit may dig in as it cuts, kicking back the workpiece.

Metallurgy and the Manufacturing Process

Understanding something about how high-speed steel and carbide router bits are manufactured may give you some insight into the various quality levels available in router bits. A lot of work goes into making a router bit, and the fact that they are so reasonably priced attests to the quantity they are manufactured in.

HSS

High-speed steel is a special type of tool steel that can work at elevated temperatures. (Common woodworking hand tools are generally made from cheaper high-carbon tool steel, which is often called water-hardening steel. Temperatures as low as 430°F can start to draw the temper of high-carbon steel — we all know the woe of burning carbon tools at the grinder. Around the turn of this century, metallurgists found that by alloying 14% to 20% tungsten into high-carbon tool steels the property of "hot hardness" could be obtained. That means that the heat-treating process is irreversible by ordinary means, and the temper of the metal can not be drawn through grinding or normal working. Metalworking cutting tools of these new alloys could be used at much higher rates of feed and speed without the edge failing, so they were dubbed "high-speed steel." However, tungsten is a rare and expensive element. Metallurgists soon found that by also alloying molybdenum (from 5% to 9.5%), the tungsten content could be reduced by approximately half.

HSS bits are manufactured in two ways: machining and investment casting. Machined bits are directly machined from bars of M-2 HSS, although M-1 is also occasionally used. M-2 is a very good HSS for it has both molybdenum (5%) and tungsten (6%). The cutting edges are created on these bits by milling flutes and relief grinding the periphery.

Investment casting has made possible the economical manufacture of HSS bits of complex shape. Although the investment-casting process dates back to the ancient Chinese and Egyptians, who used it to make coins and jewelry, it did not become commercially viable until the 1940s. In investment casting, a plastic injection molding machine is used to inject high-grade wax into an injection-molding die of the correct shape. The machine spits out plastic replicas of the desired router bit, which are then bonded onto a central wax rod called a core. Between 30 and 500 parts can be bonded onto the core, and the final assembly is called a tree. The tree is then "invested" in a heat-resistant refractory material that forms a shell around the wax models.

Once the investment shell material is hard, the wax is melted out in an autoclave. The tree is put into a special machine that spins it as the molten metal is poured. Centrifugal force ensures void-free castings. Some manufacturers also use a partial vacuum to ensure fill of the molten metal, while others use unique gates and venting techniques. Once cool, the investment material is broken away and the castings are cut off of the tree. The result is a router bit that needs a minimum of machining.

Although M-2 can be cast, it is very expensive. The tungsten readily contaminates the casting equipment, and it must be flushed with molten mild steel. Therefore bits are cast from M-52. With 4.5% molybdenum, no tungsten and 4% chrome, it just barely qualifies as a high-speed steel. The redeeming factor is that it also has 2% vanadium, which makes it very resistant to wear.

Carbide

Chemically, carbide refers to a range of compounds formed when various metals combine with carbon. The carbide in router bits is tungsten carbide, which is formed when particles of tungsten chemically combine with lampblack (carbon). Such carbide is cemented carbide, a powdered metal. Cemented carbide is made when tungsten carbide is mixed with cobalt and formed into the desired shape through pressing the "powder" in a die or extruding it. It is then put in a sintering oven and heated until the cobalt fuses the particles of tungsten carbide together.

The ideal woodworking cutter has high abrasion resistance and toughness (the ability to withstand shock). These are mutually exclusive attributes, however, and one can only be achieved at the expense of the other. Abrasion resistance refers to the ability of a particular metal to hold an edge. If less cobalt is used, the carbide can be made more abrasion resistant, but it will also become more brittle, because it is harder. Grades C2, C3 and C4 are used in router bits, and the higher the number, the greater the abrasion resistance, but the more brittle the metal. Most router bits are made from C2 or C3 carbide. While C4 is used in a few bits, it is too brittle to resist chipping at the edge in most applications. Using smaller carbide grains will also increase wear resistance, and advertisers tout the virtues of "micrograin" carbides. Don't get too excited, though, for we are only talking a decrease in particle size of between .5 and 1.5 microns.

The Cemented Carbide Products Association, a trade organization, has set voluntary standards for grading carbide, which most manufacturers adhere to. However, since each manufacturer's formula is proprietary, there is little uniformity of grades among manufacturers. Also, a particular carbide may rightfully fall into two classifications, depending on the application. All this is to say that you must trust the manufacturer to use the right carbide for any given router bit's intended application. Most manufacturers use carbides that are more than adequate. In short, let the engineers worry about what carbide to use.

To make a carbide router bit the manufacturer starts with a mild steel body. The body is made by the same methods as a high-speed steel bit — it is either machined or investment cast. Pieces of carbide are then silver brazed or copper brazed onto the faces of the flutes to form cutting edges. After brazing the carbide inserts are face ground to the proper hook angle and relief ground.

The carbide inserts are delivered polished and ready for brazing. The face of the flute in the body that the carbide is to be brazed to must be a good-quality machined surface that is free of grease and oil. The clean parts are coated with flux, and the carbide insert is set in place. The flux both removes any surface oxidation and prevents further oxidation during the brazing process.

Both the body and the carbide insert are then heated slowly by one of three methods. Braze is applied to one edge of the assembly just after its melting point is reached. It immediately melts and flows between the carbide and the steel body, forming a strong, permanent union. The most common way to heat the parts is with an oxyacetylene or oxyhydrogen torch. This method is still widely used. It works well but depends on skill to ensure complete flow of the braze and overheating, which can crystallize the braze, is a danger.

The second method is induction heating. Special machinery gives a timed induction cycle to heat the assembly to precisely the proper temperature. Induction heating is more reliable than heating by torch because it ensures that proper temperatures are reached, regardless of operator skill.

The third method is to use an oven. By this method the parts are assembled with a piece of brazing ribbon between the two surfaces — most often copper foil. The parts are then heated in an oven until the copper melts. Often the oven is filled with hydrogen, which acts as a flux as it prevents oxidation. While it sounds dangerous, it isn't — the oven is sealed and the parts actually come out looking polished.

Cutting Geometry

Router bits cut radially. To understand how they work we must first examine how tools cut in general, using the simpler example of a flat tool like a hand plane. The drawing at right shows a hand-plane blade held at 45° to the surface of the workpiece, with the relevant angles called out. The tool is ground to an angle of 30° (the grind angle), which leaves a clearance angle of 15° behind the cutting edge when the tool is held at 45° to the work (the rake angle). Clearance is necessary in a cutting tool, for without it the edge cannot attack properly.

The drawing below shows the effect of rake angle. Tool A is taking a highly positive cut, which will leave a nice finish as long as it is cutting with the grain. At this angle much less power is required, but the tendency of the edge to become a wedge, splitting along the grain in reverse grain cutting, is significantly increased. Also, the edge must be of very small cross section if the tool is to have clearance, and a thin edge is more subject to failure. Tool B is taking a 15° positive cut, and while it still raises a chip, increased force is required. However, the tendency for the wood to split ahead of the tool in reverse-grain cutting is greatly decreased, and the edge can be of much greater cross section, giving it greater strength. Tool C is taking a negative rake cut, which is of little value in woodworking. Much force is required, and the plow cut leaves an abysmal finish.

A hand plane represents a nice compromise of all these values. Furthermore, in a hand plane there are additional controls over the tendency of the wood to split ahead of the iron when cutting against the grain, namely the ability to control the mouth opening and a cap iron.

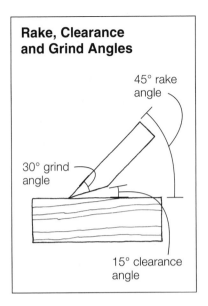

Rake, Clearance and Grind Angles

45° rake angle

30° grind angle

15° clearance angle

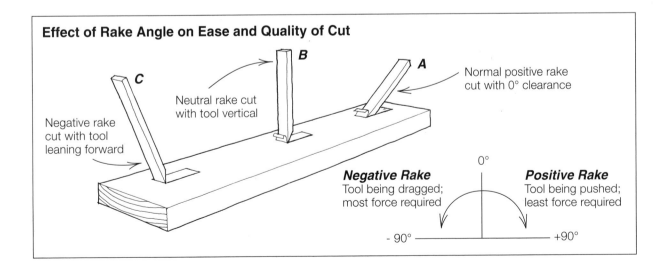

Effect of Rake Angle on Ease and Quality of Cut

C — Negative rake cut with tool leaning forward

B — Neutral rake cut with tool vertical

A — Normal positive rake cut with 0° clearance

Negative Rake
Tool being dragged; most force required

0°

Positive Rake
Tool being pushed; least force required

- 90° — +90°

By keeping the distance between the cutting blade and the sole of the plane (the mouth opening) very small, the wood is physically held down until the cutter acts on it. This arrangement can be mimicked in the router table by having a zero-clearance fence with an opening the same profile as the bit. On a plane, the cap iron breaks the chip fibers, further reducing splitting ahead of the cutter, but there are no cap irons for router bits. Instead, a higher rake angle is generally required to minimize splitting ahead of the cutting edge.

How a Router Bit Cuts

Router bits cut radially, but they follow the same basic cutting principles as the hand plane. Cutting edges equivalent to the iron are created by milling two or more flutes into a steel body. In a high-speed steel bit, the flutes become the cutting edges; in a carbide bit, flat pieces of carbide brazed into the milled flutes become the cutting edges. The drawing below shows an end view of a $\frac{1}{2}$-in. dia. carbide-tipped straight bit, with the critical angles called out.

The rake angle, which bit manufacturers refer to as the hook angle, is formed by the front face of the cutting edge and an imaginary line extending from the tip of the cutting edge through the center point of the bit. The rake angle determines the angle at which the cutting edge

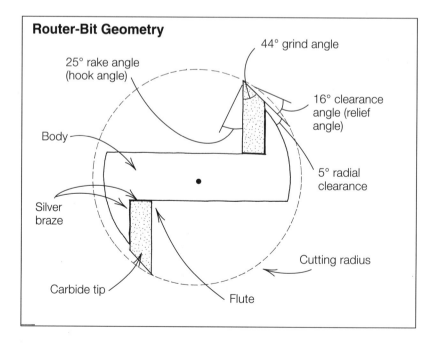

Router-Bit Geometry

25° rake angle (hook angle)

44° grind angle

16° clearance angle (relief angle)

Body

5° radial clearance

Silver braze

Carbide tip

Cutting radius

Flute

meets the workpiece and is largely controlled by how far off center the flute is milled. In this case the rake angle is 25°. The average rake angle for wood-cutting router bits is 25°. If the rake angle is too great, the wood will be more likely to split ahead of the cutting edge; if it is too small, the edge gets thin and fragile, and will wear out faster. Bits designed for cutting highly abrasive materials, such as MDF, have a rake angle of about 15º.

The clearance angle (sometimes called relief angle) is referenced to the radius the cutting edge circumscribes. It is a straight line or an arc (which is referred to as radial clearance) ground into the cutting edge and lying inside the circumscribed radius. Whether a manufacturer uses a radial grind or a straight grind for the clearance varies. A radial relief puts more strength in the cutting edge but is more costly. Many manufacturers use a radial relief for straight bits and a straight grind for profile bits. In any case the type of relief matters little in daily use; what is most important is that there be enough of it. If there is insufficient relief (less than 10°) the part of the cutter behind the point will "heel out," rubbing the work surface, rather than clearing it. Such a bit quickly overheats, and the edge fails.

For the bit in the drawing the clearance angle is 16°. Industry figures for clearance average 15° to 18° for straight grinds and around 12½° for radial relief grinds. A bit needs a minimum of 10° of clearance if it is not to heel out, but more than 20° does nothing except excessively thin the cutting edge.

Sharpening

With the exception of light touch-up of HSS bits, you should not attempt to sharpen your own bits. Leave this work to professionals. Carbide requires special grinding equipment with diamond wheels to be sharpened properly.

When a router bit is sharpened, only the face of the flute is ground, the relief is left alone. For this reason a bit gets slightly smaller in diameter each time it is sharpened. On most bits a slight loss of diameter is inconsequential, but on others it can change the size of the joint or profile. Grooves and dadoes must often be to an exact width, and sharpening may render the bit sufficiently undersized to create problems (you might be better off using cheap or HSS bits and throwing them out when they get dull. Likewise matched sets of bits may not match after a number of sharpenings. Matched sets should always be sharpened together and should be inspected and tested after each return from the grinder.

Most people start to think about sending a bit out for sharpening when it burns the wood in spots and abrades it in others, but waiting until this point is bad shop practice and greatly reduces the life of the bit. As the bit dulls, heat builds up at the edge and accelerates wear, which in turn builds up more heat, leaving the bit with a generous radius where there once was a cutting edge. When a bit like this finally gets sharpened, a lot of metal has to be ground off the faces of the flutes to bring back a sharp edge. It's best to send your bits out for grinding the minute they start to lose performance. Telltale signs are the need for greater feed pressure, increased noise level and burning.

Finding a good sharpening service can be a problem in remote areas. The "Tool Grinding" listing in the Yellow Pages is a good place to start. You might also ask local cabinetmakers or tool dealers where they send their bits to be sharpened. I generally like to look at the equipment in the shop before consigning bits to someone whose work I don't know. If in doubt, I leave only one or two bits for "test" sharpening. Pricing varies from hourly rates to per bit or even per flute pricing. I send bits to my regular sharpener via UPS and generally have them back within a week.

It is possible to stone the faces of the flutes of HSS of simple shape with a oil, ceramic or diamond stone. It is often possible to get another use in this way. After this they must either go to a sharpening service or into the dumpster depending on their price. It is often cheaper to pitch a HSS bit to than sharpen it.

Cleaning and Storage

A clean bit cuts better and lasts longer than a bit coated with pitch. As pitch builds up behind and in front of the cutting edge, the clearance angle is effectively reduced, and chip ejection is reduced as well. The bit has to work harder, and becomes dull more quickly.

There are a variety of cleaning preparations that can be used to clean bits (see Sources of Supply on pp. 114-116), and some of these purport to lubricate the surface of the bit as well. While these cleaner/lubricants can extend the time between sharpenings, they will not make a dull bit sharp. These products may contain chlorinated solvents, denatured ethyl alcohol and petroleum distillates, so you should avoid breathing them. As an alternative to commercial cleaning preparations, you can soak your bits in paint thinner and brush them occasionally with a bristle brush.

Pilot bearings (see pp. 69-73) benefit from a bit of lubrication. Here is where one of the spray lubricants can do some good. They can flow around the shields into the bearing and once the vehicle evaporates a dry lubricant is left behind. Liquid graphite lubricants, which are available at hardware stores and auto-parts stores, will also lubricate bearings well.

Router bits should be stored in their original packaging or otherwise protected, not be thrown loose in a box or drawer and allowed to roll against each other. Since I like to be able to inspect all my bits when looking for a particular profile, I drill holes just slightly larger than the bits' shank sizes in a scrap block and store my bits vertically, as seen in the photo below. That way the bits are available for inspection, they don't bang against one another, and I can carry them easily to wherever I am working.

Router-bit storage is simplicity itself: Bits stand in holes that accommodate their shank size. In this arrangement, they don't bang into each other, and they are easy to locate. Photo: Susan Kahn.

Bit Styles

There are router bits offered for every conceivable purpose—and new bits are being invented every day. I find catalogs invaluable and peruse them often for new ideas. Most of the mail-order suppliers listed in Sources of Supply on pp. 114-116 offer frequent catalogs, either free on request or at a nominal charge. Rather than discuss every type of bit on the market, I'd like to discuss the major categories.

Straight bits

Straight bits are the most basic of bits and can be used for cleaning up an edge or cutting grooves, dadoes, rabbets, mortise and tenons and inlay work. There are three common flute configurations for straight bits: straight, skewed and spiral (see the drawing on the facing page). Most straight bits have straight flutes that run parallel to the long axis, and in smaller sizes they are often solid carbide, rather than having brazed inserts. With straight flutes, the entire edge of the bit contacts the work at the same time, resulting in a certain amount of chatter. Straight-fluted bits spend a lot of time recutting debris.

Bits with skewed flutes (see the photo at left) have flutes that are milled at an angle to the axis, effectively lowering the rake angle. With these bits, although the entire edge is working at the same time, chatter is reduced because the cut starts gradually, and chips tend to be lifted out of the cut, reducing the amount of work the bit has to do.

A bit with skewed flutes cuts more smoothly than a bit with straight flutes. Photo: Susan Kahn.

Straight bits come in a vast array of sizes and configurations. From left to right: a ½-in. bit with straight carbide flutes, a ¼-in. solid carbide bit, a ⅜-in. HSS spiral bit and a ½-in. flush trim bit.

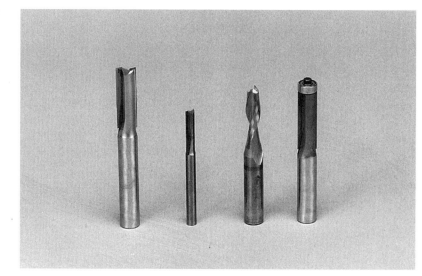

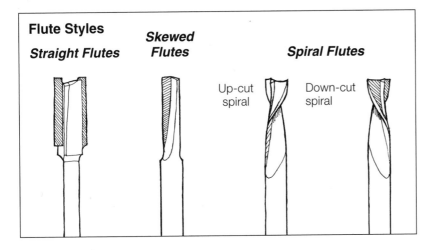

Flute Styles

Straight Flutes **Skewed Flutes** **Spiral Flutes**

Up-cut spiral Down-cut spiral

Spiral-fluted bits have helical flutes, like a twist drill. Although they are old hat in the metalworking industry, they are a relatively new discovery for woodworking. They cut far better than straight bits because the debris is pulled or pushed out of the cut, not recut by the bit, which is the case in straight-flute design. The result is a true shear cut and reduced chatter.

Spiral-fluted bits are available in up-cut and down-cut versions. Up-cut bits pull the debris toward the shank and have a right-hand twist. Down-cut bits throw the debris away from the shank and have a left-hand twist. Down-cut bits are mostly for specialized, high-tech machinery used in furniture factories. For general router-table use, an up-cut bit is best.

Spiral-fluted bits, because of their complicated shape, are almost always high-speed steel. For the most part, router-bit manufacturers are acting as retailers for these handy bits, which are really two-fluted end mills designed for metalworking. In fact, you can usually find them at a much cheaper price though industrial metalworking suppliers (see Sources of Supply on pp. 114-116).

Two extremely handy variations of the straight bit are the laminate trimmer (also called flush-trim bit) and the pattern bit. Both have pilot bearings that match the outer diameter of the bit (for a discussion of pilot bearings, see pp. 69-73), and both can be used with router tables or with hand-held routers. Laminate trimmers have a bearing on the end of the bit, and as the name implies, they are for trimming plastic laminate flush with the edge of the substrate it is glued to. They have many other purposes as well, such as trimming dovetails flush to a carcase. Pattern bits simply have the pilot bearings on the shank of the bit just above the flutes rather than on the end of the bit. They are used for following a pattern attached to the work and are immensely useful for duplicating small parts.

Profiling bits

Profiling bits mill decorative edges such as ogees or half-round molding and also can be used to make joints, such as edge glue joints or lock miters. Woodworking tool catalogs and story displays are full of profiling bits, and a good selection of profile bits will add pizzazz to your woodworking. A beginner might start with the four common profiles shown in the drawing at left.

More complex profiles can be milled using multiple-profile bits. These bits, generally of classical molding profiles, can be used to produce a vast variety of shapes by changing the height of the bit and/or the angle of the workpiece (see p. 83).

Panel-raising bits Panel-raising bits are available in horizontal and vertical configurations (see the drawing on the facing page). The horizontal type is probably easier to use, but its large diameter demands a powerful router that has speed control. Horizontal bits are typically $2\frac{1}{2}$ in. to $3\frac{3}{8}$ in. in diameter, so they require a minimum of a 3-hp router with a speed control to reduce speed to the 8,000-rpm to 16,000-rpm range, depending on diameter. (For a discussion of speed vs. bit diameter, see the sidebar on the facing page.) These bits are also available in two and three-flute configurations (sometimes listed in catalogs as two- or three-wing bits), often of European design. Because they can take only a very light cut, you'll have to make an additional pass or two to form the panel rise.

Vertical panel-raising bits can be used in routers that lack speed controls, but they require a much taller fence than supplied with commercial router tables. A shop-built fence 6 in. to 8 in. high is a must, both for safety and for good results. Brad Witt of Woodhaven has a patent on a particular type of vertical panel bit (see Sources of Supply on pp. 114-116). He also licenses others to make the bit. This bit is 1 in. in diameter and of one-piece design. It can be run at full speed in routers as small as $1\frac{3}{4}$ hp. Other companies make vertical bits that are in the $1\frac{1}{2}$-in. to 2-in. dia. range. These need more power (2 hp to $2\frac{1}{2}$ hp) and a speed control to reduce router speed to 18,000 rpm or less.

Common Profiling Bits

Roundover

Chamfer

Cove

Roman ogee

Panel-Raising Bits

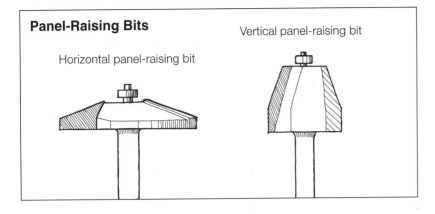

Horizontal panel-raising bit

Vertical panel-raising bit

Bit Diameter and Router Speed

The larger the bit diameter, the faster its rim will be moving. When using bits larger than 1 in. in diameter, it's important to reduce the speed of the router, so the rim speed at the cutting edge remains within safe limits. A bit that spins too fast tends to burn the work, and the potential for kickback is greater too. Speed may be reduced either by using a variable-speed router or an after-market speed-control device (see pp. 10-11).

The chart below suggests maximum allowable speeds for various router-bit diameters when cutting wood, MDF or plywood.

Bit Diameter vs. Router Speed	
Bit Diameter (inches)	**Maximum Speed (rpm)**
1 or less	20,000 to 24,000
$1\frac{1}{16}$ to 2	18,000
$2\frac{1}{16}$ to $2\frac{1}{2}$	16,000
$2\frac{9}{16}$ to 3	10,000 to 14,500
$3\frac{1}{16}$ and more	8,000 to 12,000
This information has been adapted from the Eagle America catalog.	

Matched sets

Many router-table operations call for a set of matched cutters (one is the negative profile of the other). For example, in a rule-joint set, the first cutter mills a radius and the second cuts a matching roundover, making the joint that allows a drop-leaf table to fold down.

The most common use of matched sets is in the making of cope-and-stick panel doors, where each cutter assembly is composed of two to three cutters plus pilot bearings stacked on a $\frac{1}{2}$-in. shank (see the drawing below). The sticking assembly mills a profile on the inside edges of the stiles and rails. The coping assembly copes a matching profile on the ends of the rails. (Making a cope-and-stick panel door is discussed in detail on pp. 104-107.)

Unless both profiles match exactly, the result will be mediocre at best. That's why I don't scrimp on matched sets. I buy only from first-rate suppliers who will exchange a defective set or refund my money if the profiles do not match.

Many companies offer single-cutter economy cope-and-stick sets. With these sets, the sticking cutter can be restacked on the shank in a different arrangement to make the cope cut. These cutters usually work fine, but they are not as convenient as having two separate cutters. With a matched set, changing from the stick cut to the cope cut is as easy as changing bits. With the reversible single arbor set, the operation takes much longer.

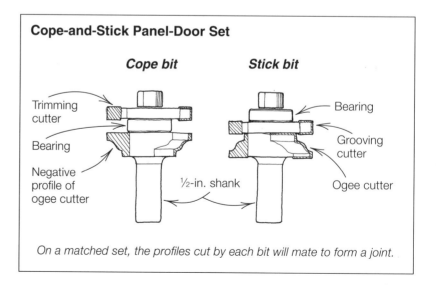

Cope-and-Stick Panel-Door Set

Cope bit   *Stick bit*

Trimming cutter

Bearing

Negative profile of ogee cutter

$\frac{1}{2}$-in. shank

Bearing

Grooving cutter

Ogee cutter

On a matched set, the profiles cut by each bit will mate to form a joint.

While reversible sets are fine for symmetrical shapes such as a quarter-round, they can not be used for shapes that are asymmetrical end to end, such as an ogee. A so-called ogee reversible cutter will not yield a true ogee, but rather a sort of sine-wave shape.

Guiding the Work through the Cut

The most basic way to guide a workpiece through a cut is by sliding it along a fence (see pp. 36-42). That works fine for straight cuts, but what if you want to mill a curved edge or reproduce an irregular shape several times? That is where pilot bearings and guide bushings come to the rescue.

Pilot bearings

Pilot bearings allow radial guidance of the workpiece so the edge can be any shape, so long as it is of greater radius than the bearing. The drawing on p. 70 shows three typical bearing-guided setups.

A pilot bearing is a shielded ball bearing that rides over (or in some cases under) the cutter. A curved work surface can be guided by this bearing just as if it were a straight surface guided by a fence. Sometimes part of the workpiece itself rides against the pilot bearing; other times a template may be attached to the workpiece and the bearing will ride against the template. Templates may be attached above or below the workpiece, depending on the circumstances. The template may also double as a fixture to control the work.

If the bearing is guiding off the workpiece directly, always begin with a smooth edge on the workpiece, since your work will only be as true as the surface the bearing makes contact with. Most pilot bearings are of small diameter, so it does not take much irregularity in the work surface to cause a wavering profile. Edges that are to be milled should be planed or sanded smooth before routing begins.

Heavy, hogging cuts invite disaster. The quality of the cut will suffer, and the risk of the workpiece getting away from you will greatly increase. Since you can't use featherboards with pilot-bearing work, you have to depend on your own strength to hold the work steady against the bit. The heavier the cut, the more difficult this is.

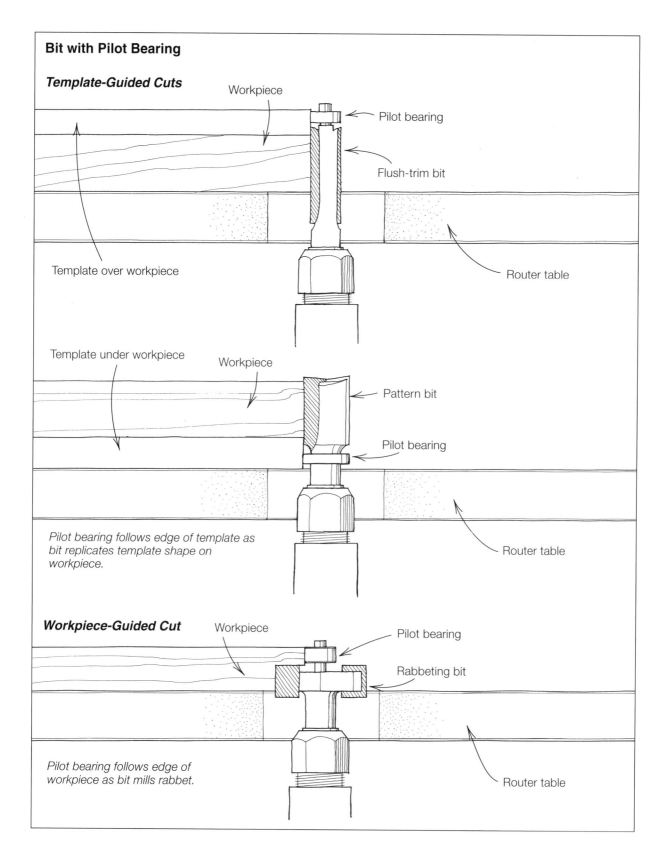

Bit with Pilot Bearing

Template-Guided Cuts

Workpiece

Pilot bearing

Flush-trim bit

Template over workpiece

Router table

Template under workpiece

Workpiece

Pattern bit

Pilot bearing

Router table

Pilot bearing follows edge of template as bit replicates template shape on workpiece.

Workpiece-Guided Cut

Workpiece

Pilot bearing

Rabbeting bit

Router table

Pilot bearing follows edge of workpiece as bit mills rabbet.

In pilot-bearing-guided work, you won't be able to start the cut safely and smoothly unless you use a starting pin (see p. 16). The starting pin is positioned just to the right of the cutter, on the infeed side of the router table (see the drawing below). The workpiece is placed against the starting pin, pivoted into the cutter until the edge of the workpiece touches the pilot bearing, then slid to the left until the edge no longer makes contact with the bit. Some people like to add another pin on the outfeed side of the table so the workpiece can be pivoted smoothly off the bit without inadvertently rounding the corner. At least a starting pin is necessary for safe pilot-bearing work.

Whether or not to hold the work in a fixture is largely a function of the size of the workpiece. Large workpieces, where the operator has good leverage, may be routed without a fixture. Small pieces almost always need a fixture. A properly designed fixture (see the sidebar on p. 72) always makes pilot-bearing work safer and usually delivers better, more consistent quality.

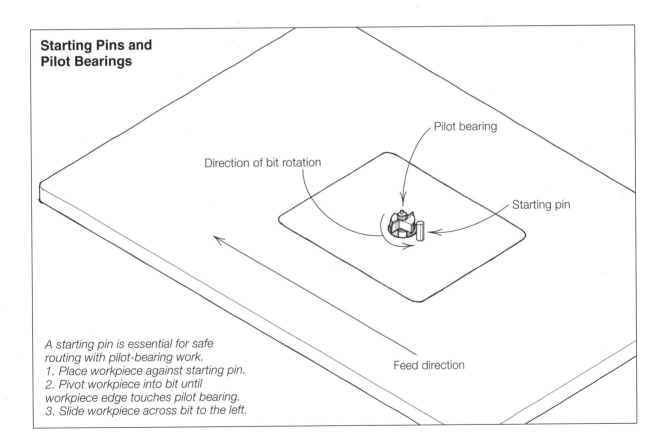

Starting Pins and Pilot Bearings

Pilot bearing

Direction of bit rotation

Starting pin

Feed direction

A starting pin is essential for safe routing with pilot-bearing work.
1. Place workpiece against starting pin.
2. Pivot workpiece into bit until workpiece edge touches pilot bearing.
3. Slide workpiece across bit to the left.

*F*ixtures for Pilot-Bearing Work

A well-designed fixture for pilot-bearing work holds the workpiece securely, affords the operator good leverage for control of the workpiece and puts the operator's hands in a safe relationship to the router bit. Additionally a fixture may serve as a pattern that the pilot bearing follows to mill a specific shape or profile. Such fixtures are well suited to the serial production of identical small parts.

A fixture can often be improvised. Grabbing the workpiece with a clamp will afford leverage and keeps the operator's hands away from the bit (see the top photo at right). In a pinch, a scrap block can be wire-nailed or taped with double-sided tape to the workpiece to serve as a fixture.

There are also commercial fixtures, such as RGT Handler (see the bottom photo at right). This OSHA-approved fixture is useful in a wide variety of pilot-bearing work.

If you don't find a commercial fixture that suits your needs, you can make your own (see pp. 74-75 for a vacuum fixture you can build). Making fixtures is an art unto itself — no two woodworkers approach it the same way, and there is always more than one solution to a fixturing problem.

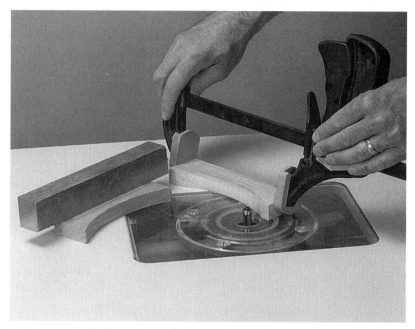

Two improvised fixtures: At left, a scrap block taped to the workpiece with double-sided tape can be used to guide it past the bit. At right, a simple clamp grips the workpiece.

RGT Handler is a commercially available fixture that holds the work securely, affords the operator good control over the workpiece and puts the operator's hands out of the way of the bit.

Pilot-bearing work is safe as long as certain precautions are taken. The cutter should always be protected by a guard (see pp. 50-51 for one you can make), and the hole in the router baseplate should be close to the diameter of the bit. If necessary, use starting pins to start and end the cut, feed the work in the proper direction (see pp. 80-81), and take light cuts.

Templates Templates (sometimes called patterns) can be made of virtually any stable, workable material, such as plastic, solid wood, plywood or MDF, and common pattern thicknesses are ¼ in., ½ in. and ¾ in. Templates can often be designed to double as a fixture (for an example, see the fixture for milling the top rail for an arched panel door on pp. 111-113).

Templates generally ride above the workpiece, but can run below in some circumstances. With the template on top you would generally use a flush-trim bit; with the template on the bottom you would use a special straight bit called a pattern bit. Both of these bits can mill a curved edge that is square to the face. A template eliminates the need to bring the edge to a smooth finish, for the pilot bearing follows the template and not the work itself. The work is simply bandsawn slightly oversize, affixed to the template and routed to a final edge.

There are many ways to attach the template to the workpiece—nails, screws or clamps are the simplest. Double-sided tape is good for one-time or low-production use. When using double-sided tape it is important to hold the workpiece and template together in a vise or clamp for a few seconds to achieve a proper bond. Otherwise, the tape can fail in the middle of the cut. However, clamping may make the two difficult to separate once the milling is completed.

Another way to hold the template to the workpiece is by vacuum. Vacuum fixtures are well suited for volume production. They are easy to build (see the sidebar on pp. 74-75), and they don't require special material—just plastic, MDF or plywood for the pattern, a pressure-sensitive gasket, plastic tubing, fittings and a way to generate a vacuum. A vacuum pump works well, but these are quite expensive. You can also use a simple device that attaches to any air compressor. It uses a venturi to create a partial vacuum—generally around ¾ atmosphere (25 in. of mercury). Though not as effective as a vacuum pump, it is sufficient for most purposes.

Making a Vacuum Fixture

The vacuum fixture described here will hold a workpiece for pilot-bearing work, and can be adapted to guide-bushing work (see pp. 76-77) as well. For either setup, begin by making the template. You can use ¼-in. thick plastic (Plexiglas works well), ½-in. MDF or ½-in. high-quality plywood. Cut it to the exact shape of the piece to be milled and smooth its edges. If you use MDF or plywood, seal all surfaces with several coats of white shellac or lacquer to prevent air leakage. You can also attach handles at this point, if you like.

If your fixture is to be used with a pilot bearing, drill a hole at a convenient location for the vacuum fitting and place pressure-sensitive gasketing material around the perimeter of the pattern (ordinary pressure-sensitive weatherstripping works fine, and this material is available at most hardware stores and home centers). You'll generally need a minimum of 10 sq. in. of area inside the gasket to hold the workpiece securely, depending on the efficiency of the vacuum source, and the porosity of the fixture and workpiece. I have made fixtures with as little as 5 sq. in., but with these I took light cuts.

Gasket the perimeter of the fixture with pressure-sensitive weatherstripping. (The hole will receive the vacuum fitting.)

Screw the vacuum fitting into the top of the fixture and attach the hose. Since pipe threads are tapered the fitting will screw into an accurately drilled hole. A sealant such as glue on the thread will seal the fitting against leakage.

With the gasket in place, screw the vacuum fitting into the hole in the top of the pattern and attach the vacuum hose. Since pipe threads are tapered, the fitting will screw into an accurately drilled hole. A little white or yellow glue applied to the threads before assembly will seal the joint against leakage, yet allow the fitting to be replaced easily. Now place the assembled fixture on the workpiece and turn on the suction. You are ready to rout.

If the fixture is to be used with a guide bushing, you will have to redesign it somewhat. Using 1-in. thick MDF, locate the fitting in the side with a vacuum channel elbowing up to the top side of the jig, as shown in the drawing below.

The finished vacuum fixture can be used with a bearing-guided bit.

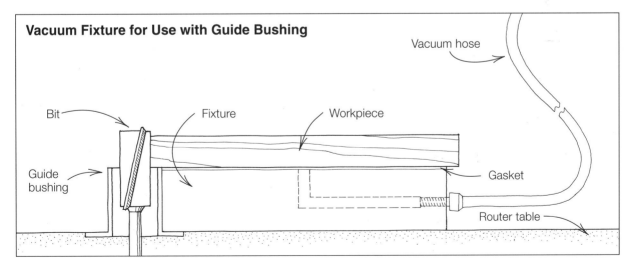

Vacuum Fixture for Use with Guide Bushing

Vacuum hose

Bit

Fixture

Workpiece

Guide bushing

Gasket

Router table

Guide bushings

Guide bushings are tubes that fit into the router baseplate and are concentric to the router collet. They are available in a wide range of sizes to accommodate larger and smaller bits and a variety of situations (see the photo below). Guide bushings can do the same things as pilot bearings, but in a router table the guide bushing will always be below the cutting area of the bit. A typical guide-bushing setup is shown in the drawing on the facing page.

Most router manufacturers make their own guide bushings, and one bushing often comes with the router. The problem is that the router manufacturer's system may not be compatible with the after-market baseplate you choose for mounting your router in a table. Many baseplates are not designed to accept guide bushings at all. The baseplates that are designed to accept guide bushings are generally made for the Porter-Cable system.

Working with guide bushings is similar to working with pilot bearings (see pp. 69-73). Cutter rotation is counterclockwise, and work should be fed into the direction of cutter rotation (from right to left as you face the router). A starting pin is essential and a exit pin may be helpful. For safety, never work with an unguarded bit larger than ¾-in. tip diameter, and hold small parts in a fixture.

If you are using a guide bushing, the pattern must be attached below the workpiece. That means you'll need a slightly different jig to hold the two together (see the drawing on p. 75).

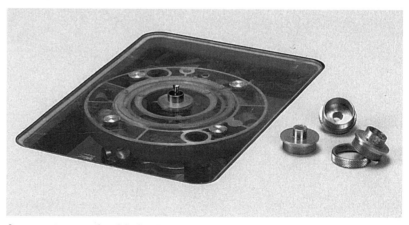

An assortment of guide bushings.

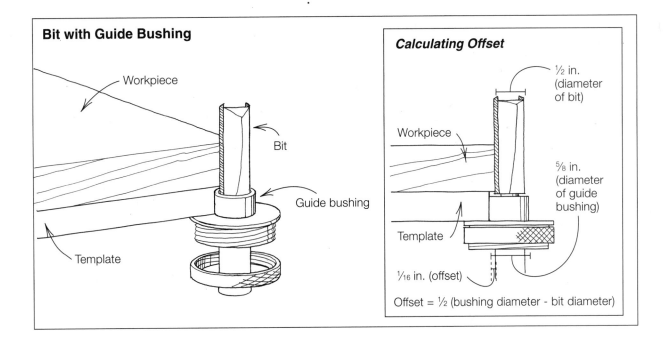

Bit with Guide Bushing

Workpiece

Bit

Guide bushing

Template

Calculating Offset

½ in.
(diameter
of bit)

Workpiece

⅝ in.
(diameter
of guide
bushing)

Template

¹⁄₁₆ in. (offset)

Offset = ½ (bushing diameter - bit diameter)

Calculating offset Most router-table work is done with a ⅝-in. dia. bushing because it has a center bore large enough for a ½-in. dia. router bit shank to pass through. However, because the guide-bushing diameter is larger than the bit diameter, the workpiece will end up larger than the template that the bushing is following. In sizing the template you need to compensate for this discrepancy, generally by making the template smaller than the desired size of the finished workpiece. How much smaller should it be? This difference is called offset, and corresponds to half the difference in diameter between the bit and the guide bushing, as shown in the detail drawing above. If you are using a ⅝-in. dia. bushing with a ½-in. dia. bit, the offset is ¹⁄₁₆ in. For an example of how offset must be taken into account in setting up cuts with a hand-held router, see pp. 31-35. The same principle applies in router-table work.

CHAPTER 4
Techniques

The router table can be one of the most versatile tools in the small shop, for with it you can do anything from joinery to architectural millwork. This chapter focuses on the types of operations you can do with the router table, with an emphasis on practical techniques that are of value in the average shop. In your own work you will be able to build on these basic techniques to achieve more complex projects of your own design.

Four such projects appear in this chapter—a drawer (see pp. 91-93), a finger-jointed box (see pp 101-102), a cope-and-stick door frame (see pp. 106-107) and an arched-panel door frame (see pp. 111-113)—as examples of how different router-table techniques can be used in combination to produce a finished piece of work.

With router-table work, as with many other machine-tool operations, proper setup is the key to success. Don't try to rush this process. If set-up is given short shrift, your safety and the quality of your work will be compromised. Powerful forces are generated by a bit spinning at sev-

Traditional cope-and-stick raised-panel doors can be made on the router table using just a few different cutters and setups.

Strategically located featherboards hold the workpiece down on the router table and tight against the fence.

eral thousand rpm, and you will have to counterbalance these forces through the use of fences, fixtures or other hold-downs and guards, properly prepared stock and the way you feed the workpiece into the bit. I always allow 10 to 20 minutes for setup—enough time to plan for the details of the operation. It is easy to be lured onto the rocks by the sirens of speed, but don't succumb, even if small jobs, requiring only a couple of feet of milling, take longer to set up than to run.

In all router-table operations, it is critical to feed the workpiece in the proper direction (see the sidebar below) and to maintain complete control over the piece as you move it past the cutter. Featherboards (see the photo at left and the discussion on pp. 51-52) and other commercially available guiding devices such as the wheeled hold-downs shown in the top drawing on the facing page should be used wherever possible to keep the work flat to the table and tight against the fence.

*F*eed Direction and Speed

Feed direction is important to consider when you are setting up for a cut, particularly with large-size bits. With the router upside-down in the table, the bit spins counterclockwise. The safe way to feed the workpiece is into the cutter, i.e., to the left if you are standing at the front of the table (with the fence behind the bit), as shown in the bottom drawing on the facing page.

Reverse-direction feeding, usually called "climb cutting," should be avoided. If you feed the workpiece to the right, the

cutter will tend to pull the workpiece toward itself, possibly dragging your fingers along with it. Climb-cutting cuts are also rougher and not as easily controlled; the bit may grab and throw the workpiece.

As you plan the feed direction, also consider the grain of the workpiece. Generally it's best to rout with the grain, but that is not always possible. If you must rout against the grain and have done everything possible to ensure a smooth cut, yet are still having problems, here are two tricks to remedy the situation. One is to take several passes, making the final a light one in the neighborhood of $\frac{1}{64}$ in. to $\frac{1}{16}$ in. The other is to make a series of plunge cuts by pivoting

the work off of either end of the fence into the cutter at intervals about $\frac{1}{2}$ in. apart. It is often good to set the fence a little forward (or the bit a little lower) before doing this so that you are not plunging quite to full depth. Now run the work as you normally would; because the grain is in short sections it will not tear out.

On the router table, light cuts, a steady feed and firm pressure work best. Use enough featherboards to hold the workpiece flat against the table and fence, and let the cutter do the work. If the router bogs down (you'll know by a change in the sound), you are feeding too fast and/or taking too heavy a cut. Recommended feed rate

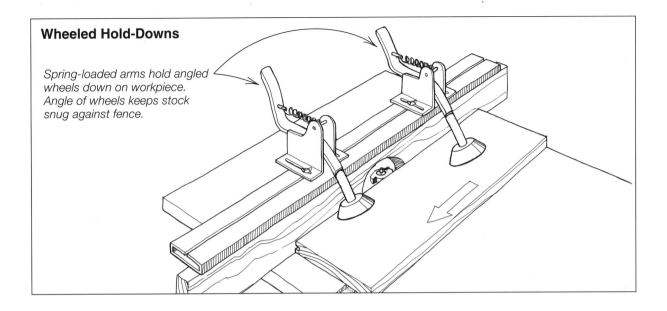

Wheeled Hold-Downs

Spring-loaded arms hold angled wheels down on workpiece. Angle of wheels keeps stock snug against fence.

for a sharp ½-in. dia. two-flute cutter is between 11 ft. and 12 ft. per minute. For larger-diameter bits and/or more flutes, the feed rate should be reduced.

Most people tend to feed stock at the wrong speed. The result of fast feeding is that wood breaks out excessively in front of the bit and the surface finish of the cut suffers. One of the advantages of a router is that its high speed leaves an excellent finish, but overfeeding increases the distance between cuts, giving the surface a scalloped look. On the other hand, feeding the work too slowly may burn some woods (like cherry) and the cutter can dull prematurely.

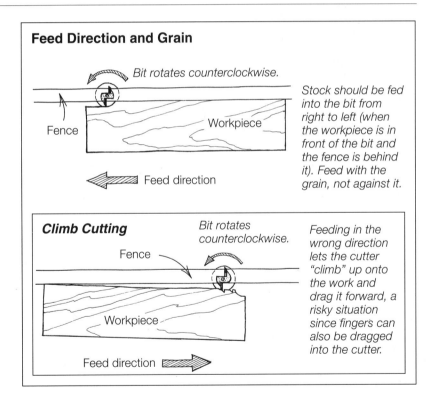

Feed Direction and Grain

Bit rotates counterclockwise.

Fence

Workpiece

Feed direction

Stock should be fed into the bit from right to left (when the workpiece is in front of the bit and the fence is behind it). Feed with the grain, not against it.

Climb Cutting

Bit rotates counterclockwise.

Fence

Workpiece

Feed direction

Feeding in the wrong direction lets the cutter "climb" up onto the work and drag it forward, a risky situation since fingers can also be dragged into the cutter.

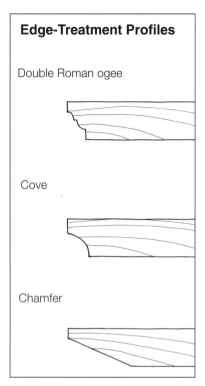
Edge Treatments

Look closely at just about any piece of furniture and you will find examples of edge treatments you can create with your router table. Table tops, drawer fronts and door edges all regularly feature some kind of molded edge. Even the rule joint used on most drop-leaf table designs is actually an edge treatment.

Simple edge treatments

The widespread popularity of the router in nearly every woodworking shop has led to a nearly limitless variety of router bits for creating decorative edges. You can use some of the basic bits shown in Chapter 3 to make effective edge treatments to dress up your furniture projects. Following are several other edge-treatment options.

Ogee bits are perhaps the most common edging bits you will find. In addition to the Roman ogee shown in the drawing on p. 66, there are double Roman ogees, classical ogees, ogees with fillet and many other lesser-known variations. Changing the diameter of the bearing that guides these bits can also alter the profile of the finished edge.

Cove bits are shaped like a quarter-circle and come in a variety of sizes. They can be used alone or in combination with other cutters to establish many different profiles.

Chamfering bits cut chamfers, one of the simplest edge treatments. These bits are available in a wide variety of angles from as little as 11° to 45°. Various chamfer angles can also be used to cut multi-sided boxes: For example, a hexagon can be constructed by using a 30° chamfer, an octagon with a 22½° chamfer, and so on.

Fingernail bits are oversized cutters with a profile that is part of an ellipse or an oval (see the drawing at left). You can use fingernail bits to create the soft, elegant, edges that are common to many large classic table designs.

Half-round (bull-nose) bits (see the drawing at left) give you the same treatment that you would obtain by making two passes over a roundover bit.

Beading bits have the same shape as roundover bits, but with a slightly smaller-diameter bearing. The smaller bearings create extra flat faces on either side of an ordinary rounded edge. Edge-beading bits come in a wide variety of styles. The most common put a bead along with a small reveal that adds both character and dimension to an edge.

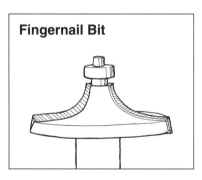
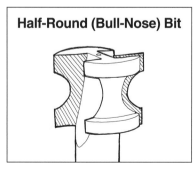

Corner (side-beading) bits are similar to beading bits, but require two passes—one along the edge and the other along the face of the workpiece. The result is a bead profile that wraps the corner. This detail is often used on reproduction Shaker-style peg board.

Complex edge treatments

Once you have worked with simple edge treatments, you may feel the need to expand your repertoire into more complex profiles. One way to do this is by using a multiple-profile bit. Multiple-profile bits have a very complex profile. You use them in one or more passes: If you change the height of the bit relative to the workpiece, only certain parts of the bit cut on each pass. You can also cut different profiles in two or more pieces of stock and then assemble them into one large molding, as shown in the drawing at right. With this approach, the profiles you can cut are limited only by your imagination and ingenuity. Another way to achieve complex profiles is by positioning the workpiece at an angle to the bit. Changing the angle allows subtle adjustments in the profile.

The best way to gain confidence with edge treatments is to try as many as you can. Experiment with cutting depth and combinations until you have built up a vocabulary that suits the furniture and projects you are most likely to tackle.

Sometimes very simple changes can make a big difference in the look of the piece. For example, the two panels in the drawing below differ only in the location of the chamfer. The first panel, with its top edge chamfered, has a solid, massive feel. The second panel, with its bottom edge chamfered, looks thinner and more delicate.

Edge Treatments and Panel Design

Chamfer on top lends weighty feeling to panel.

Chamfer on bottom yields lighter, more delicate look.

Creating a Complex Molding with a Multiple-Profile Bit

Cut a profile on the larger piece of stock (1), then raise the bit and cut a different profile on the smaller piece (2). Glue the two together (3).

Handling Panels

The router table is a great tool for cutting decorative or functional profiles into the edges of panels. This broad grouping of cuts includes such diverse operations as cutting rule joints in drop-leaf tables, cutting a pleasing profile around the perimeter of a tabletop and making raised panels.

For end-grain cuts, a few words of warning are in order. End-grain cuts are common in router-table work, but they are difficult because of tearout as the cut is completed. When the cutter breaks free of the edge, it tends to break the wood along the grain adjacent to the cut. In end-grain work the cut must always be backed up to prevent splintering around the break-out. With panels this is generally best done by using a squared-off piece of scrap as a push block or a quick and dirty miter gauge. The push block should be the same thickness as the panel so it can pass under the featherboards. Cuts across the end grain of a panel should be made before cuts with the grain.

For the cuts with the grain, the setup is much the same as with other operations of this type. Featherboards, however, can be employed only on the fence to hold the panel down, not on the router table to hold the panel against the fence, so the operator will have to maintain pressure against the fence. This is not usually a problem, given the size of most panels.

Panels that are large enough to hang off the front of the table usually need a bit of outboard support. With panels I prefer the support afforded by long infeed and outfeed tables, as opposed to turning the fence across the table. Bowing on glued-up panels may also be a problem, and it is best to run the work with the bow down so that the work is not pushed up off the cutter in the middle of the panel.

Very large panels present special problems. At a certain point it is often better (in terms of both safety and quality of cut) to do edge treatment with a hand-held router, unless the bit is too large to be used safely in that tool, as would be the case with panel-raising bits. Fortunately few raised panels are larger than the capacity of most router tables. Most profiling bits, such as ogees, quarter-rounds or coves, are no more than $1\frac{3}{4}$ in. in diameter, and these can be used in a hand-held router quite well. As a rule of thumb I will not use bits over 2 in. in diameter in anything but a table with a router equipped with a speed control. Even bits in the $1\frac{1}{16}$-in. to 2-in. range should be run at a slower speed than usual, say about 18,000 rpm. For a discussion of recommended speeds of bits with bits of various diameters, see p. 67.

Edge treatment of panels

1. Make the end-grain cuts, backing up the workpiece with a squared-off piece of scrap to prevent splintering as the bit emerges from the cut.

2. Make the cuts along the grain.

3. The finished panel.

Moldings

One common use of the router table is in the making of all types of molding, both for furniture and for architectural use. Not only does the router table do this job better than historical methods (planes), it also allows you to mill an infinite variety of profiles in just about any type of wood. Commercial moldings are very expensive, yet moldings can be made most economically on the router table. I milled all of the molding for our home and saved myself a lot of money. I also had the opportunity to create complicated moldings that would have been difficult to obtain commercially.

Until quite recently there were few choices if you needed some special moldings for your project. You could use a shaper and expensive cutters to make your molding, use a series of hand planes to arrive at the profile you might need or buy ready-made molding close to the shape you wanted. Now a nearly unlimited supply of molding profiles is available from your router. Just about any source you'll find for router bits will have a selection of profiles that will give your projects exactly the effect you need. In my own work with moldings I've found the following types of cutters very useful. These are shown in the drawings on the facing page.

With the router table you can mill complicated moldings that would be hard to obtain commercially.

Face Molding Bits

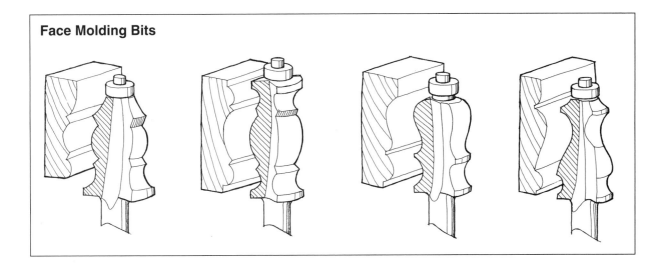

Face molding bits are available in many sizes and shapes, including classical molding bits. They shape all or part of the face of the stock into some of the most frequently used profiles in woodworking. They come in handy for room trim and furniture.

Molding systems are sets of bits designed to produce an almost limitless varitey of molding shapes. These often lack guide bearings and are intended for use only on router tables.

Accurately dimensioned stock is essential for making moldings on the router table (see the sidebar on p. 88). When smaller sections are ripped from a larger plank, they often twist somewhat. Milling moldings requires plenty of featherboards to lock work down securely on the table and against the fence. If the stock is a little bowed and/or twisted, the featherboards will flatten it as it passes by the cutter. The fence opening should also match the bit profile as closely as possible. Use a zero-clearance fence (see pp. 38-41) in difficult work such as curly figured woods or milling against the grain.

For moldings of larger section, bow can also be a problem. It is generally best to run the stock with the bow down so that the work cannot be forced up off of the bit and to use shorter infeed and outfeed tables. For this reason it is sometimes better to run the work across, rather than the length of, the typical center-mounted router table. With an offset router you can run the stock in the normal manner. Any residual twist and bow can be pressed out when the completed molding is applied to to the finished work.

Molding Systems

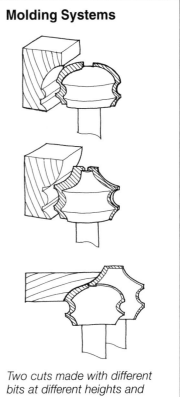

Two cuts made with different bits at different heights and fence settings produce a profile impossible to obtain with either cutter alone.

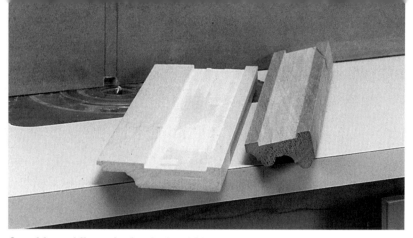

On wide moldings the back should be relieved so that the finished moldings will sit flat on uneven surfaces.

It is good shop practice to relieve the back of wide moldings so they will naturally sit flat on uneven surfaces (see the photo above). This can usually be done most effectively with a rabbeting bit or a large-diameter (⅝-in. or greater) straight bit. Typical relief is between ⅛ in. and ¼ in. deep. If you are using a rabbeting bit, you have to set the bit to less than the distance afforded by the pilot bearing. Relieving the back requires an additional setup and pass on the router table, but is well worth the effort, especially on architectural moldings.

Stock Preparation

If you wish to make moldings, you must begin with stock that is square and of consistent cross section. Stock of inconsistent thickness and width will be difficult to feed smoothly past the featherboards, and a poor surface finish will be the result. You can prepare your stock yourself or buy stock that has been surfaced at the lumberyard.

To prepare your own stock for moldings, start with straight-grained stock and joint it to establish a true face and edge. Then rip it to a slightly oversize cross section, and use a thickness planer to bring the section to exact size. The result is high-quality material that will feed well and yield first-rate molding.

If you buy your lumber in quantity, having it surfaced on two sides (S2S), is often worth the cost, which in Ohio, where I live, is between $80 and $120 per thousand board feet. While the yard is at it, also have one edge "straight-line ripped" with a special saw (stock prepared this way is referred to as S3S). Prices vary greatly, but typically having one edge straight-line ripped ranges from nothing to an additional $80 to $120 per thousand board feet. Many lumber dealers stock S3S material. For smaller orders it is frequently worth the extra cost to get S3S material. If you try to do this work yourself on a small jointer and thickness planer, it will literally take you days to surface and true one edge of a batch of rough boards. You may be spending more in time than you are saving in dollars.

Routing molding

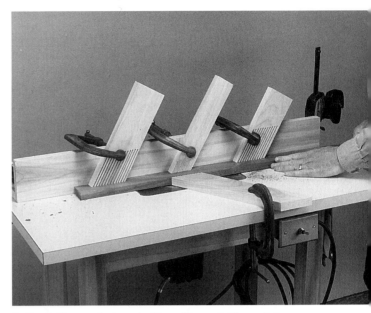

1. The basic setup for making molding includes featherboards to lock work down securely on the table and against the fence, and a fence that matches the bit profile as closely as possible.

2. Push the workpiece halfway through the cut. In a good setup, the stock can be pushed halfway, then pulled the rest of the way from the outfeed side of the table. Featherboards ensure that there will be no telltale ridge on the workpiece.

3. Pull the workpiece through the remainder of the cut. If working alone, you can walk to the outfeed side and pull the work the remaining distance, or a helper (if you have one) can take over at midpoint, leaving you free to fetch the next piece of stock.

4. The finished molding.

Cutting Joints on the Router Table

Not too long ago, making carcase joints on a router table required multiple passes or a special fixture. Now there are special bits that can make carcase joints in a two-step process. Shown in the drawing below are two examples of joint-cutting bits: a lock-miter bit, which can make post assemblies and even glue joints, and a lock-joint bit for making drawers. In both cases one piece is run past the bit face down and the mating piece is run vertically past the same cutter to create an interlocking joint.

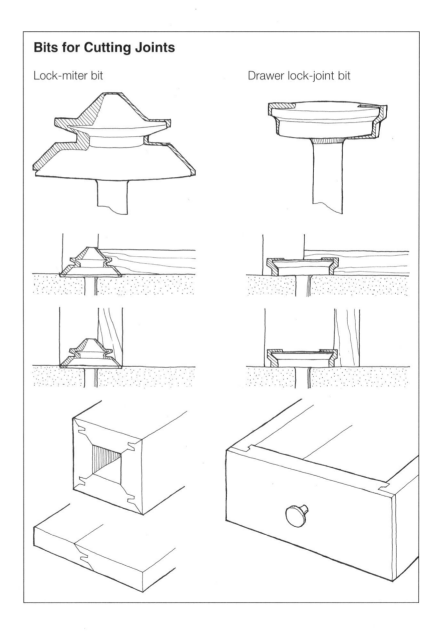

Bits for Cutting Joints

Lock-miter bit

Drawer lock-joint bit

Making drawers

Making drawers is one of the most basic tasks in a woodworking shop, and I am constantly in need of them myself for storage, household built-ins and even kitchen cabinets. In fact, it seems I can never make them fast enough. The router is a good friend in drawer making. Equipped with a ¼-in. spiral-fluted straight bit, it makes the groove that holds the drawer bottom.

Drawers made in the traditional manner, with a solid wood bottom, have a back that is narrower than the rest of the drawer, so that a solid wood bottom can be slid under it and into the grooves that run along the sides and the front (see the photo below). The grain of the bottom piece runs across the drawer, and the back is nailed or screwed to the bottom edge of the back, with some play allowed in the front groove to allow for expansion and contraction of the wood with seasonal changes in humidity.

It is often convenient to make the sides and backs of such drawers from ½-in. plywood, and for this, too, the router table is a godsend. Because of plywood's alternating grain, dovetails are not of much use, but you can use the drawer lock-joint cutter, described on the facing page, to cut locking corner joints in plywood. The drawer side is cut across the grain, with the workpiece vertical against the fence, and then the drawer front is cut across the grain, with the workpiece flat on the table. The photo-essay on pp. 92-93 details the steps.

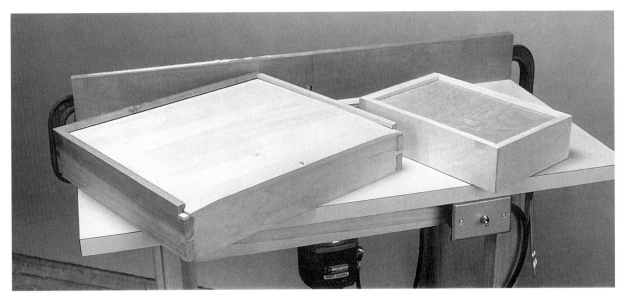

A traditional drawer (left) and a plywood drawer (right).

Making a drawer

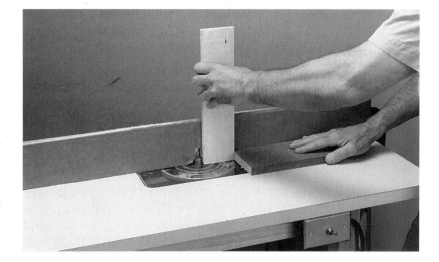

1. With a lock-joint cutter in the router, make the end-grain cut on the side of the drawer, using a quick and dirty miter gauge to push the workpiece through the cut.

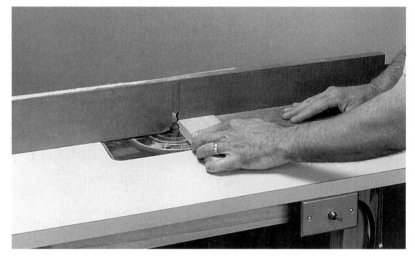

2. Make the end-grain cut on the drawer front, again using the quick and dirty miter gauge to push the workpiece through the cut.

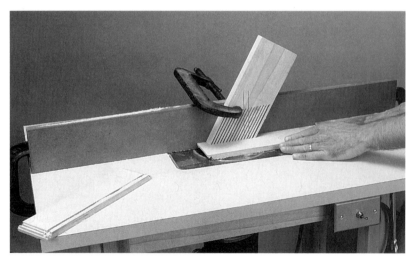

3. Rout the grooves in the sides and bottom, using a spiral-fluted straight bit.

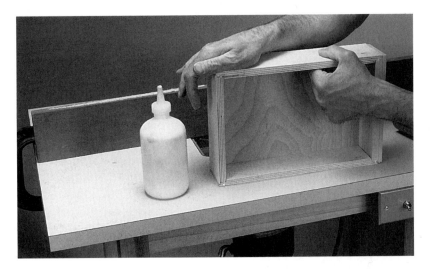

4. Glue the drawer together.

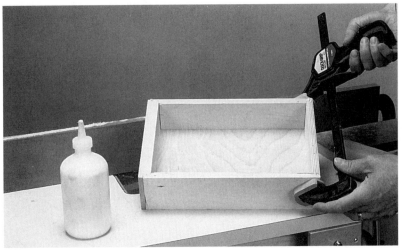

5. Clamp the joints tight until the glue dries.

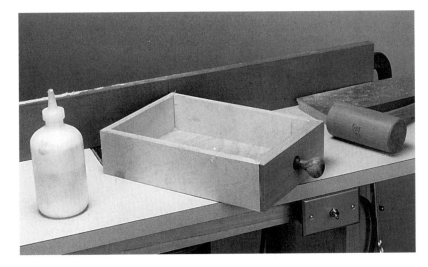

6. With the addition of a knob, the drawer is complete.

Grooves, Dadoes, Rabbets and Sliding Dovetails

The router table is immensely useful for all types of grooving operations. Variations on the basic groove, shown in the drawing below, include dadoes, rabbets and sliding dovetails. A groove is a trough that runs with the grain, whereas dadoes are troughs that run across the grain. (In plywood, MDF and other man-made sheet goods, however, this distinction is largely moot.) In carcase construction a dado is called a housing if it runs the full width of the board or panel it is to trap. A rabbet is a groove along the edge or end of a board or panel. Fillisters (a variation of the rabbet) are merely a rabbet on the back of the work, but parallel to the face of the work. They derive from sash work.

Rabbets are frequently encountered in carcase and frame construction. The same basic setup is used regardless of grain direction, but the workpiece needs a backup block with end-grain cuts to avoid tearout as the bit emerges from the edge of the work at the end of the cut. The backup block can be a simple piece of squared-off waste stock used as a push block or a quick and dirty miter gauge (see p. 48). The block

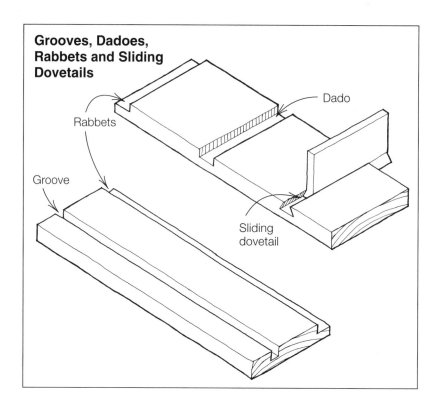

Grooves, Dadoes, Rabbets and Sliding Dovetails

Rabbets

Dado

Groove

Sliding dovetail

should be the same thickness as the work so it will pass under the featherboards. If one, or both, adjoining edges are to have a profile, the rabbet should be cut before the profiling to avoid having to mill special profiled backing blocks.

For milling rabbets, grooves and dadoes, nothing beats an up-cut spiral bit (see p. 65). Of course in a router table everything is upside-down, so an up-cut bit really pulls the debris downward, away from the cutting flutes. Dust and dirt end up below the surface of the table, where they can be collected.

The setup is simple: Just place the fence at the distance from the cutter that will yield the desired cut. On rabbets this usually means that the fence will be partially over the bit, so you should use a close-fitting or zero-clearance fence for good results. To cut a rabbet, feed the workpiece from right to left at a steady rate (see the photos below).

Routing a rabbet

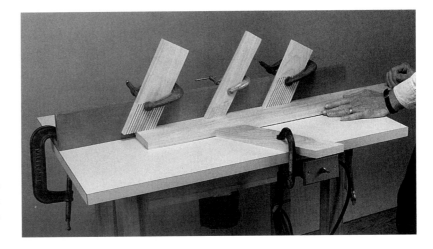

Featherboards hold the workpiece down against the table and against the fence as it is pushed at a steady rate of feed over the cutter. A similar setup can be used for other grooving cuts with the grain.

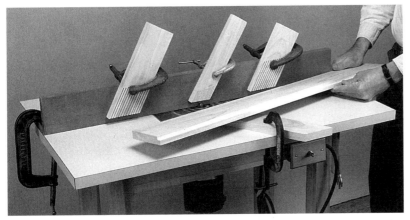

The finished rabbet.

For grooves the fence is set back from the bit by the amount the groove will be offset from the edge. As with all cuts along the grain, use plenty of featherboards and, if possible, run the work with the bow down.

For most situations you use a bit the same diameter as the groove you want to cut, but occasionally you need to mill a groove that is between bit sizes. In this case you make one pass, using the smaller bit, then move the fence back the desired distance from the bit and make a second pass. For reasons of safety, always move the fence away from the bit for succeeding passes. Moving the fence toward the cutter so as to bring the groove nearer the edge of the work will result in a climb-cutting situation (see the detail drawing on p. 81), with possible dire consequences. If you move the fence nearer the cutter, you will have to feed the work from the opposite direction.

Stopped cuts

Carcase construction often requires stopped rabbets or stopped grooves. These cuts, which stop short of the full length or width of the workpiece, are more difficult to mill than through grooves. For stopped rabbets (see the photo-essay on the facing page) fewer featherboards must be used, and the workpiece must be pivoted into the bit. For stopped grooves (see the photo-essay on p. 98), featherboards can not be used at all, and the work must be pivoted down onto the bit. Drawing pencil lines on the featherboard or fence at the edges of the bit to demarcate its working area will help in starting and stopping the cut at the right time. Stopped cuts are more dangerous than normal cuts along the grain. Always be sure your fingers are positioned in such a way that they cannot be dragged into the cutter if kickback should occur.

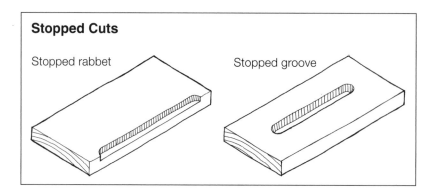

Stopped Cuts

Stopped rabbet

Stopped groove

Routing a stopped rabbet

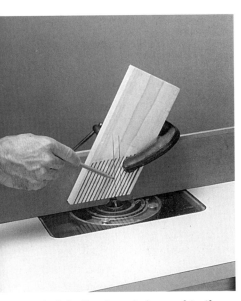

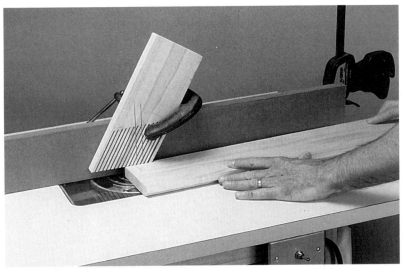

2. Pivot the workpiece into the bit at the start of the cut.

1. A featherboard clamped to the fence will hold the workpiece down on the table but the operator must hold the work against the fence. Pencil lines on the featherboard mark the cutting area of the bit.

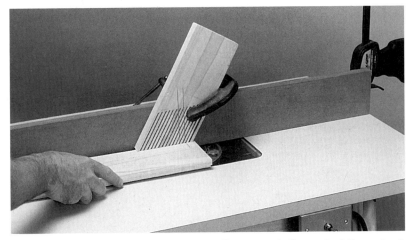

3. Slide the workpiece over the bit until you reach the end of the cut, at which point you pivot it away from the bit.

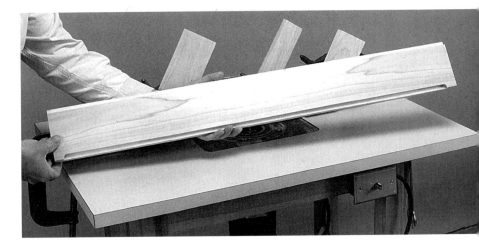

4. The finished stopped rabbet. Depending on the mating piece, you can leave the corners rounded as they are milled by the bit, or square them up with a chisel.

Routing a stopped groove

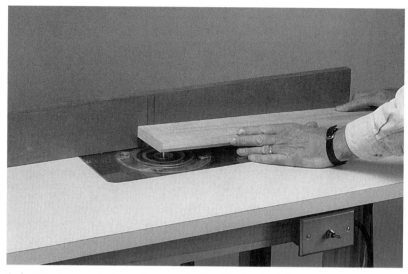

2. Lower the workpiece down onto the bit to start the cut.

1. For stopped grooves featherboards cannot be used, so you have to hold the workpiece firmly against the table and the fence. Set the fence at the required distance from the bit; pencil lines on the fence mark the cutting area.

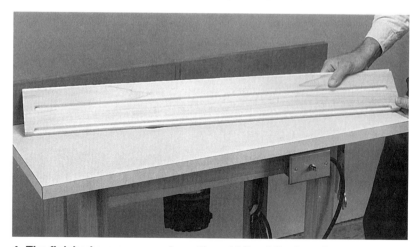

3. At the end of the cut, raise the workpiece up off the bit.

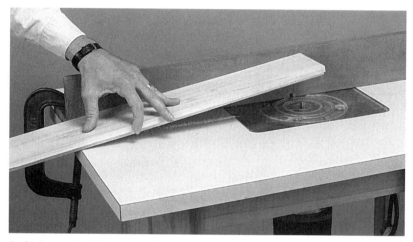

4. The finished groove runs down the middle of the board.

Sliding dovetails

Another variation of the groove is the sliding dovetail, and this is easy to mill on the router table. However, instead of milling it in one pass, it is better to mill out the center portion first with a spiral-fluted straight bit, then widen it to the desired profile with a dovetail bit (see the photo below left). Trying to make a blind cut (a cut the full width of a bit which is not open at one edge) will generally lead to problems. Chips cannot be evacuated from dovetail-shaped cuts and the bit overheats quickly, leading to premature dulling or even breakage.

If the sliding dovetail has the same profile as the dovetail bit, it can be milled in just two passes. But if it is to be wider than the bit, you will have to make additional passes, resetting the fence. If you make all your passes on the side farther from the fence, you can feed the workpiece in the normal manner, from right to left, as described in the sidebar on pp. 80-81. However, if you mill the side closer to the fence, you have to feed in the opposite direction (from left to right) to avoid a climb-cutting situation.

How you cut the mating dovetailed piece depends on whether the cut will be on the edge of the board or on the end of the board. Cuts along the edge of a board may be made on the table saw. You can also cut this piece on the router table, using the same dovetail bit that cut the groove. Cuts on the end of a board may be milled with the aid of a miter-slot-guided tenoning jig, as shown in the photo below right.

Routing a sliding dovetail joint

1. After milling a groove with a straight bit, mill the dovetail profile with a dovetail bit.

2. With the workpiece held in a miter-slot-guided tenoning jig, mill the mating piece with the same dovetail bit.

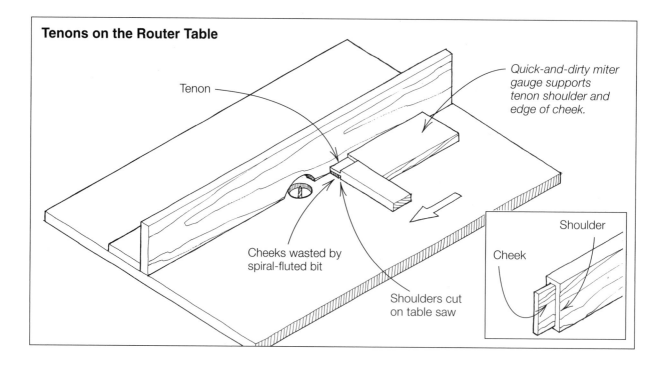

Tenons on the Router Table

Tenon

Quick-and-dirty miter gauge supports tenon shoulder and edge of cheek.

Cheeks wasted by spiral-fluted bit

Shoulders cut on table saw

Shoulder

Cheek

Tenons

There are several ways to cut tenons on the router table. One is to cut the shoulders of the tenon on a table saw, then rout out the cheeks as shown in the drawing above, using a $\frac{1}{2}$-in. or $\frac{5}{8}$-in. dia. spiral-fluted bit for best results. Another is to employ a tenoning jig in the miter slot of the router table and use a spiral-fluted bit. Results here are better if the shoulders are cut first on the table saw, but they do not have to be. If you don't have a table saw, cut the shoulders with a sharp knife to prevent tearout, then rout the cheeks with a sharp spiral-fluted bit.

The router table is not particularly good for making mortises. Since the cut is completely blind, it is difficult to start and stop the mortise exactly where you want to. Hold-downs that would prevent the work from getting away from you are also difficult to set up. Other tools (such as the hollow mortise chisel) or the hand-held router are better for making mortises.

Dovetails and Finger Joints

Unless you are using a manufactured dovetail jig, the router table is not particularly good for dovetailing. Small dovetails for drawers and boxes can be done with the Incra Pro or JoinTECH systems (see pp. 42-44), both of which come with detailed instructions on cutting dovetails. However, these systems are not adequate for dovetailing large carcases. A simple jig that cradles the corner of the box at a 45° angle to the router table can be built to cut mock dovetails, but remember that the mock dovetail is mainly a decorative feature. A finger joint gives more long-grain glue area is therefore a much better joint.

Making a finger-jointed box

My Stanley router plane has always needed a home for all its parts and cutters, and it seemed fitting, in an ironical sort of way, to use the router table to make a finger-jointed box to hold this traditional but still useful tool. The box has a rabbeted top that slides in grooves in the carcase (see pp. 94-96 for how to cut rabbets and grooves). To cut the finger joints, you can use a modified version of the bushing-guided miter gauge described on pp. 50-51 with a jig taped to it with double-sided tape. The jig, shown in the drawing below, is no more than a pin that locates each finger as it is cut so that the next finger will be cut at a precise distance away.

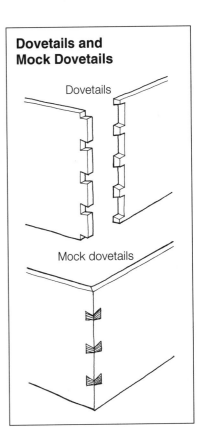

Dovetails and Mock Dovetails

Dovetails

Mock dovetails

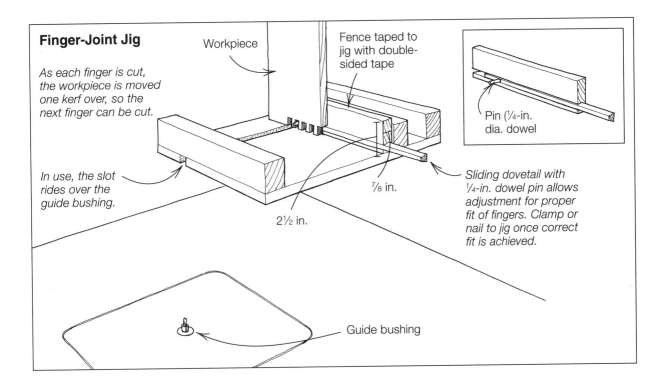

Finger-Joint Jig

As each finger is cut, the workpiece is moved one kerf over, so the next finger can be cut.

Workpiece

Fence taped to jig with double-sided tape

In use, the slot rides over the guide bushing.

Pin (¼-in. dia. dowel

⅞ in.

2½ in.

Sliding dovetail with ¼-in. dowel pin allows adjustment for proper fit of fingers. Clamp or nail to jig once correct fit is achieved.

Guide bushing

Start with boards that are cut to final size. To mill a side board, align the edge with the pin (with the outside of the box against the jig) and rout the first finger. Then drop that kerf over the pin, make another cut, and move the resulting kerf over the pin. This process continues until all the fingers are milled across the box. While the sides of the box start against the pin, the first cut on the ends of the box (the outside should face away from the jig) starts even with the edge of the bit. That way the edges will mate when the joint is assembled. (You could also clamp a side and an edge together, offset by a kerf width, and mill the two together.)

Finger-jointed box

1. Cut the finger joints with a ¼-in. spiral-fluted bit. Each cut indexes onto a ¼-in. pin, giving perfect spacing of the fingers.

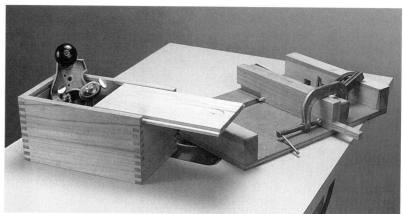

2. The finished box.

Cope-and-Stick Operations

The terms ""cope" and "stick" date from the days of hand-tool joinery. To "stick" a molding, you positioned a suitable plank between bench dogs and cut the desired profile with a molding plane. Cuts were always made with the grain. The freshly planed shape could be ripsawn from the board and be "planted" by nailing or gluing in place on the work.

Today, a shaper or router is generally used to mill a profile on the long grain of square or rectangular stock. With machine work, one is not restricted to milling wide boards, so strips of suitable width can be ripped first on the table saw and milled directly. For this work, all you need are a fence and a bit of the suitable profile.

The term "cope" comes from the installation of architectural molding. Until the early part of this century, such moldings were quite wide. When wide moldings meets at an inside or outside corner, cutting the ends of each to a 45° angle is fine if the room is square, but rooms rarely are, even in modern buildings. The traditional solution (see the drawing below) is to cut the first piece square to the corner, then "cope" the molding profile in the end of the mating piece with a coping saw. A coped joint will fit without gaps even if the room itself is out of square.

Today, we refer to the "cope" as the mirror image of the "stick." By definition, the cope cut is made in end grain, whereas the stick cut is made with the grain. In frame-and-panel doors we can use this technique to produce a cope-and-stick joint.

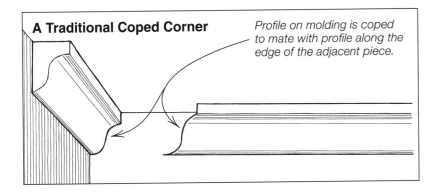

A Traditional Coped Corner

Profile on molding is coped to mate with profile along the edge of the adjacent piece.

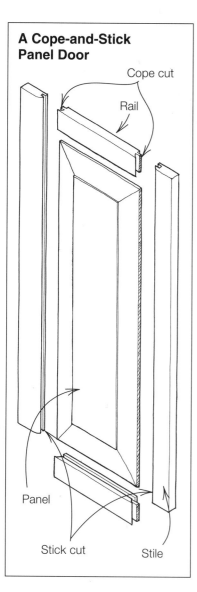

A Cope-and-Stick Panel Door

Cope cut

Rail

Panel

Stick cut

Stile

The drawing at left shows a typical cope-and-stick panel door. Originally the rails and stiles for such doors were assembled with mortise-and-tenon joinery. In the Georgian period, the molded edge around the panel and the groove was stuck with hand planes. The stuck profiles of the stile and rail were cut back to the depth of the groove before the mortise and tenon were cut, and the stuck profiles on both the stile and the rail were mitered at the corners for a perfect fit. Later, during the Greek Revival Period, the molded edge around the groove was planted, which made hand-tool construction much simpler.

The frame for a frame-and-panel door can be made on the router table (see the photo-essay on pp. 106-107) by using a set of matched cutters (see the drawing on p. 68). Such sets are variously called stile-and-rail sets or cope-and-stick sets. The inside edges of the stiles and the rails are stuck with a groove (Step 1 on p. 106). At the same time the cutter also mills the molded profile (parroting the planted or stuck moldings of old) leading up to the groove. The ends of the rails are coped with the mirror image of the stuck profile, the effect being a stubby mortise and tenon joint. Because of the perfect match of the milled surfaces, the joint works quite well. This joint is used on modern interior and exterior doors as well as in cabinetry.

When setting up for sticking the inside edges of stiles and rails, it's a good idea to have extra stock on hand to allow for test cuts, as well as milling and machining goofs. First set the cutter height by eye (Step 2), then align the fence (Step 3). This can be done by placing a steel rule against the bearing and snugging the fence up to the rule. Now make trial cuts to ensure that the bit is at the right height. Most cope-and-stick sets are designed for ¾-in. stock to be run face down and are set at the correct height when the groove is about ⅛ in. from the back of the stock. (This puts the back of the groove ⅝ in. from the face, which is the thickness of most panels.)

Work is run face side down on the table. It is wise to pick the face based on grain orientation as you fetch each new piece of stock for sticking so the cutter will be laying the grain down as much as possible, but artistic considerations such as bookmatching the stiles may preclude this. For most jobs, however it is possible to orient the most pleasing grain to the face side and orient the edge such that the cutter is laying grain down.

In most situations end-grain cuts can be carried out before side-grain cuts. This keeps the edges of the workpiece square until coping is completed, thereby allowing them to be backed up with a square block taped with double-sided tape to the miter gauge or a squared-off waste block—the quick and dirty miter gauge (see p. 48). When making cope-and-stick panel doors, however, it's often more convenient to cut and mill all the material required for the job, then cut and fit the stiles and rails to match the cabinet face-frame openings. The length of the rail often has to be "adjusted" for proper fit. Therefore sticking is generally carried out before coping.

The right end of the top rail in the drawing on the facing page copes fine with standard backing-block techniques, but the left will not be backed up properly, and splintering at the break-out will be the result. The solution is to back up the inside edge of the rail with a special profiled backing block when it is against the miter gauge (Step 4 on p. 107). You can make this block by sticking a short, narrow length of scrap with the coping bit. The scrap should be about 1 in. wide and the same thickness as the stile and rail material.

In all router-table operations the work must be fed into the cutter (see the sidebar on pp. 80-81). Because sticking usually involves a relatively long, narrow workpiece, the work needs as much support as it can get as it passes by the bit and over the table insert. For this reason it is a good idea to use a zero-clearance fence (see pp. 39-41) and to make the opening in the baseplate around the bit as small as possible. Most operations greatly benefit from having dust evacuation (see p. 53). Carrying away the dust saves the cutter from having to recut waste, so it operates cooler.

In cross-grain or end-grain operations it is also often convenient to employ the fence. In many jobs, such as rabbets or panels, it may already be in place and set properly, and moving the fence would be a nuisance for it is needed in the next operation—sticking the edge. For cope-and-stick work, such as panel doors, the fence is a convenient way to position the workpiece before it passes through and after it exits the cutter. The problem is that the fence is seldom parallel to the miter slot. Setting the fence in correct juxtaposition to the cutter and parallel to the miter slot is a nightmare at best. Therefore it is better to use a wraparound miter gauge that guides off the fence itself (see p. 47) or a quick and dirty miter gauge, which also guides off the fence (see p. 48). Since the wraparound miter gauge is shop built, it may be run through the cutter and of itself back up a cope cut. If you do not want to dedicate a wraparound miter gauge to each bit you will be making cope cuts with, you can attach a strip of scrap with double-side tape to the leading edge for each new coping operation. The quick and dirty miter gauge is so quick to make that a new one can be made for each situation.

**Making a cope-
and-stick door
frame**

1. Stick the inside edge of
the stiles and rails, with the
workpiece face side down on the
table. Complete the cuts with the
aid of a pushstick, keeping your
hands well clear of the bit.

2. Adjust the height of the
coping cutter to the newly
milled stiles and rails.

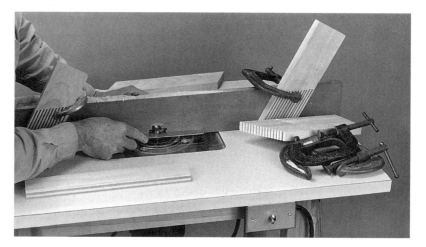

3. Align the fence to the cutter
by snugging it to a steel rule
held against the bearing, and
make a test cope cut in a piece
of scrap to ensure that the cutter
is at the correct height. Readjust
as necessary. Then use this
setup to stick a backing block.

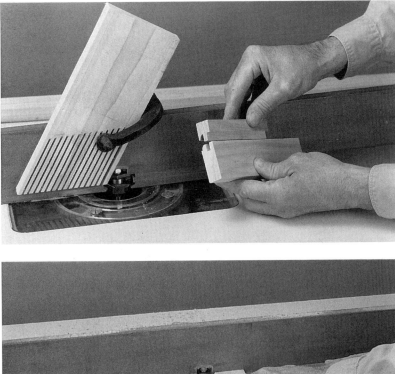

4. Install a length of backing block in preparation for coping the ends of the rails. The backing block will prevent splintering at the end of the cope cut.

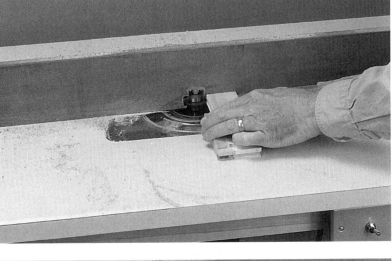

5. Make the cope cut in one pass. Double cutting may result in a loose fit.

6. The finished joint.

Raised Panels

A raised panel floats in the grooves along the stiles and rails. The purpose of this construction is to allow for expansion and contraction across the width of the panel without splitting the door or affecting its size, which is fixed by the stiles and rails. The key is to have the edge of the panel be a snug sliding fit in the groove so that it can float, but not rattle.

Horizontal vs. vertical panel-raising setups

To make raised panels on the router table you will need a panel-raising cutter (see pp. 66-67). Two types—horizontal and vertical—are available, and each has its advantages and disadvantages. With horizontal panel-raising bits, the panel is run horizontally, with the face down on the table and the edge against the fence. They generally require less setup than vertical bits, and most have a pilot bearing for running arched panels. If you have a correctly made panel to use as a model, all you have to do is put the edge against the pilot bearing and raise the bit until it just touches the rise. Now place the fence well forward of the bearing and take the first pass. Move the fence back successively until on the last pass the panel edge touches the bearing. If you are guiding off the pilot bearing you will have to start with the cutter low and raise it on successive passes. This will require care on the final pass not to make the edge too thin, which would yield a panel that would rattle in its frame.

The concept of the vertical panel-raising bit has been around for a long time and comes to the router table from shapers. It is so called because the panel is held vertically during milling, with the face against the fence and the edge on the table. The advantage of the vertical panel-raising bit is that it can be of much less diameter so that less power is needed and higher speed can be used. Vertical panel-raising bits have some disadvantages, too. They generally require an additional light pass for a good finish. If heavy cuts are taken, the bits will chatter, especially the 1-in. dia. bits. Vertical bits require a little more setup, such as a special high fence and featherboards positioned to press above the terminus of the rise. If the bit has a bearing, the fence is adjusted to it with a steel rule. If there is no bearing, adjustment is by trial and error. Finally vertical panel-raising bits can only be used on rectangular panels. Arched panels must be done with a horizontal bit.

All panel bits, vertical or horizontal, require three to five passes, and the fence or bit height must be reset each time. A light final pass will make for a superior finish, especially on the cuts across the grain. Light cuts are especially important when working off of pilot bearings. Heavy cuts make pilot bearing work uncontrollable.

In conclusion, the choice whether to use a vertical or a horizontal bit will be dictated by the shape of the panel and the horsepower of your router more than anything else. The photo-essays that follow show an arched panel door milled with a horizontal bit and a rectangular panel milled with a vertical bit.

Raising an arched panel with a horizontal cutter

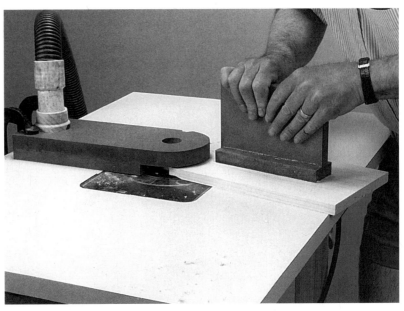

1. Cope the ends of the panel first, guiding it along the pilot bearing with the aid of a fixture attached to the panel with double-sided tape. A shop-made guard with dust-collection pickup shields the horizontal panel-raising bit.

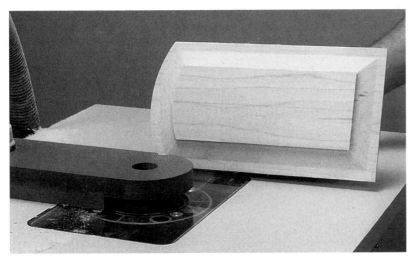

2. The finished panel.

Raising a rectangular panel with a vertical cutter

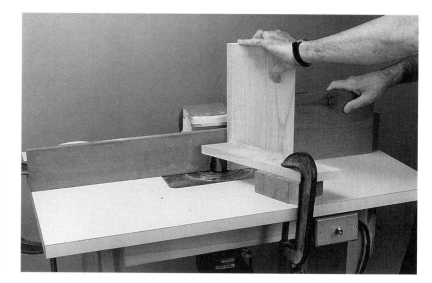

1. Raise the ends of the panel, using a piece of scrap the same thickness as the panel as a backing block and pushstick. A featherboard clamped to a riser block presses the panel square against the fence above the terminus of the rise.

2. Raise the sides of the panel, again using a backing block/pushstick.

3. The finished raised panel.

An arched frame-and-panel door

Arched panel doors can add a custom decorative touch on kitchen cabinets, as a center door in the cubbyhole of a desk and elsewhere in your house, and you can make them in whatever wood and size you want. They make an interesting break from straight lines. As shown in the six-step photo-essay that begins below, the frame for an arched panel door can be made quickly on the router table by first shaping the rough bandsawn arch with a pattern and a flush-trim bit, then sticking the inside edge with a sticking cutter and finally coping the ends of the rails. When an arched panel (see the bottom photo on p. 109) is inserted in the frame, the door is done.

Making an arched frame

1. With a vacuum fixture (see pp. 74-75) atop the roughly bandsawn blank, rout the edge of the the arched top rail with a flush-trim bit. (In this photo, the guard has been removed for clarity.)

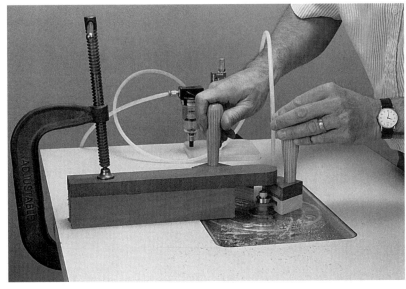

2. Stick the groove and profile on the inside edge of the arched top rail. The stiles and the bottom rail have been stuck in normal fashion, using a fence.

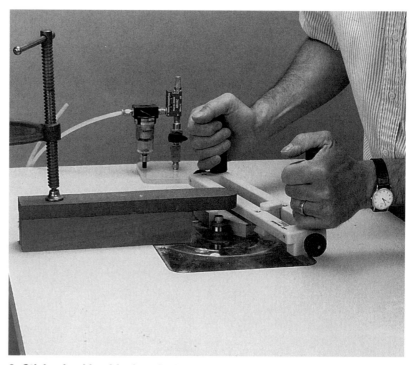

3. Stick a backing block to facilitate the coping of the end of the arch. This backing block was bandsawn to the same radius as the panel. It will both hold the arch end square and back up the end of the cut. During sticking, the block is being held by the RTG Handler (see p. 72).

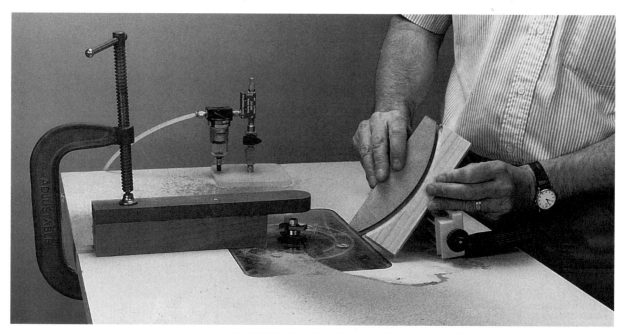

4. Install the backing block in the arched rail to facilitate coping.

5. Cope the end of the arch with backing block in place, using a quick and dirty miter gauge to push the arched rail past the bit.

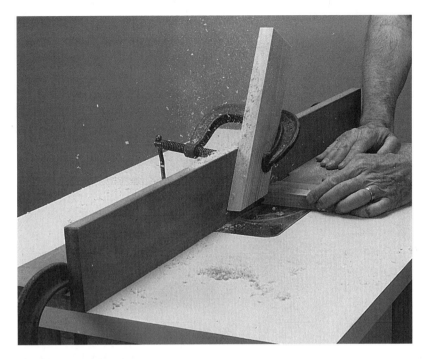

6. The finished frame, partially disassembled to show the joinery. The piece in the middle is the backing block, which can be used to cope another arched rail.

SOURCES OF SUPPLY

The following companies sell routers and router-related equipment, including, bits, tables, fences and other accessories.

Amana Tool Co.
120 Carolyn Blvd.
Farmingdale, NY 11735
(800) 445-0077
(516) 752-1300
FAX (516) 752-1674
Router bits

American Saw & Manufacturing
301 Chestnut St.
E. Longmeadow, MA 01028
(800) 628-3030
(413) 525-3961
Bit lubricant

Beall Tool Co.
541 Swans Rd. NE
Newark, OH 43055
(800) 331-4718
(614) 345-5045
Router accessory for making wood threads

Black & Decker
701 East Joppa Rd.
Towson, MD 21286
(800) 762-6672
(410) 716-3900
FAX (800) 245-8308
Black & Decker, Elu and De Walt routers

Buckeye Saw Co.
P.O. Box 46857
Cincinnati, OH 45246-0857
(800) 543-8664
FAX (513) 860-0578
Router bits

Cascade Tools, Inc.
P.O. Box 3110
Bellingham, WA 98227
(800) 235-0272
FAX (800) 392-5077
Router bits and accessories

CMT Tools
5425 Beaumont Center Boulevard
Suite 900
Tampa, FL 33634
(800) 531-5559
(813) 886-1819
FAX (813) 888-6614
Routers, tables, bits, accessories

Constantine's
2050 Eastchester Rd.
Bronx, NY 10461
(800) 223-8087
(718) 792-1600
FAX (800) 253-9663
Routers, tables, bits, accessories

Eagle America
P.O. Box 1099
Chardon, OH 44024
(800) 872-2511
(216) 286-7429
FAX (800) 872-9471
Routers, tables, bits, accessories

FS Tool Corp.
71 Hobbs Gate
Markham, ON
Canada L3R 9T9
(800) 387-9723
(905)-475-1999
FAX 905-475-0347
Router bits

Enlon Import Corp.
17709 East Valley Blvd.
City of Industry, CA 91744
(800) 888-9697
(818) 935-8888-
FAX (818) 935-8889
Router bits

Garrett Wade
161 Avenue of the Americas
New York, NY 10013
(800) 221-2942
(212) 807-1155
Routers, tables, bits, accessories

Grand Tool Supply Corp.
U.S. Highway 46 and Huyler St.
Teterboro, NJ 07608
(800) 342-8665
(201) 342-6900
FAX (201) 288-7090
Spiral bits (end mills)

Grizzly
East of Mississippi River:
2406 Reach Rd.
Williamsport, PA 17701
(800) 523-4777
(717) 326-3806
FAX (800) 438-5901

West of Mississippi River:
P.O. Box 2069
Bellingham, WA 98227
(800) 541-5537
(206) 647-0801
FAX (800) 225-0021
Routers, tables, bits, accessories

Hartville Tool and Supply
940 West Maple St.
Hartville, OH 44632-9652
(800) 345-2396
FAX (216) 877-4682
Routers, tables, bits, accessories

Highland Hardware
1045 N. Highland Ave.
Atlanta, GA 30306
(800) 241-6748
(404) 872-4466
FAX (404) 876-1941
Routers, tables, bits, accessories

Hitachi Power Tools USA
3950 Steve Reynolds Blvd.
Norcross, GA 30093
(800) 706-7337
(404) 925-1774
FAX (800) 925-0547
Routers, bits, accessories

Integra Tooling
21 Beacon Dr.
Port Washington, NY 11050
(800) 633-6312
(516) 767-2340
FAX (516) 944-5618
Router bits

International Carbide & Engineering
100 Mill St.
P.O. Box 216
Drakes Branch, VA 23937-0216
(800) 424-3311
FAX (804) 568-3412
Router bits

JoinTECH, Inc.
P.O. Box 790727
San Antonio, TX 78279
(800) 619-1288
(210) 377-1288
FAX (210) 377-1282
JoinTECH positioning system

Keller & Co.
1327 "I" St.
Petaluma, CA 94952
(800) 995-2456
(707) 763-9336
Dovetail jig

Kreg Tool Co.
P.O. Box 367
Huxley, IA 50124-0367
(800) 447-8638
FAX (515) 597-2354
Router bits, accessories

Lee Valley Tools
2680 Queensview Dr.
Ottawa, Ontario K2LB 8H6
Canada
(613) 596-0350
FAX (613) 596-0373
Routers, tables, bits, accessories

Leichtung, Inc.
4944 Commerce Parkway
Cleveland, OH 44128
(800) 542-4467
(216) 831-6191
FAX (216) 464-6764
Routers, tables, bits, accessories

Leigh Industries Ltd.
P.O. Box 357
1535 Broadway St.
Port Coquitlam, B.C.
Canada V3C 4K6
(604) 464-2700
FAX (604) 464-7404
Leigh dovetail jig

Magnate Business International
1930 S. Brea Canyon Rd., #170
Diamond Bar, CA 91765
(909) 861-1185
FAX (909) 861-2766
Router bits

Makita U.S.A.
14930-C Northam St.
La Mirada, CA 90638
(714) 522-8088
FAX (714) 522-8133
Routers, tables, bits, accessories

Micro Fence
11100 Cumpston St. #35
North Hollywood, CA 91601
(800) 480-6427
(818) 761-1433
Precision router edge guide

MLCS, Ltd.
P.O. Box 4053
Rydal, PA 19046
(800) 533-9298
(215) 938-5067
Router tables, bits, accessories

W. Moore Profiles, Ltd.
18 Montgomery St.
Middletown, NY 10940
(800) 228-8151
(914) 341-1924
FAX (914) 343-7056
Custom router bits

NuCraft Tools
P.O. Box 513
Clawson, MI 48017
(800) 971-5050
(810) 548-2380
Cast-iron router table

Phanton Engineering
1122 South State St., #21
Provo, UT 84606
(801) 377-5757
FAX (801) 377-1668
Custom bits, spindle-making device

PMS Products
285 James St.
Holland, MI 49424
(800) 962-1732
(616) 786-9922
FAX (616) 786-9130
Bit lubricants

Porta-Nails, Inc.
P.O. Box 1257
315 North 17th St.
Wilmington, NC 28402
(800) 634-9281
(910) 762-6334
FAX (910) 763-8650
Cast-aluminum router table

Porter-Cable
P.O. Box 2468
4825 Highway 45 N
Jackson, TN 38302-2468
(901) 668-8600
Routers, tables, bits accessories, Omni dovetail jig

Racal Health & Safety
7305 Executive Way
Frederick, MD 21701
(800) 682-9500
(301) 695-8200
FAX (301) 695-4413
Airstream, Airlite, Airmate dust helmets

Ridge Carbide Tool Co.
595 New York Ave.
P.O. Box 497
Lyndhurst, NJ 07071
(800) 443-0992
(201) 438-8778
FAX (201) 438-8792
Router bits, custom router bits

Rousseau Co.
1712 13th St.
Clarkston, WA 99403
(800) 635-3416
(509) 758-3954
FAX (509) 758-4991
Table inserts

S-B Power Tool Co.
4300 West Peterson Ave.
Chicago, IL 60646
(800) 815-8665
(312) 286-7330
FAX (312) 794-6615
Skil and Bosch routers and bits

Sandaro Industries
Boston St.
Middleton, MA 01949
(508) 750-7304
Lubricants

Sprayway, Inc.
484 Vista Ave.
Addison, IL 60101-4468
(708) 628-3000
Bit lubricant

Taylor Design Group
P.O. Box 810262
Dallas, TX 75381
(214) 484-5570
FAX (214) 243-4277
Incra Jig and accessories

The Tool Club
1026 Superior Ave.
Baraga, MI 49908
(800) 486-6525
(906) 337-0516
Inlay tool for routers

Trend-lines
375 Beacham St.
Chelsea, MA 02150
(800) 767-9999
(617) 884-8882
FAX (617) 889-2072
Routers, tables, bits, accessories

Fred M. Velepec Co., Inc.
71-72 70th St.
Glendale, NY 11385
(800) 365-6636
(718) 821-6636
FAX (718) 821-5874
Router bits

Vermont American
11403 Blue Grass Parkway
Louisville, KY 40299
(800) 626-2834, ext. 1407
(502) 266-1407
Routers, tables, bits, accessories

Wesley Tools Ltd.
346 Maple
Westbury, NY 11590
(800) 397-6867
(516) 338-5555
FAX (516) 338-4706
Router bits

Whiteside Machine Co.
4506 Shook Rd.
Claremont, NC 28610
(704) 459-2141
FAX (704) 459-1252
Router bits

Wisconsin Knife Works
2710 Prairie Ave.
Beloit, WI 53511
(800) 225-5959
(608) 365-9581
FAX (608) 365-4917
Router bits

Woodcraft
210 Wood County Industrial Park
P.O. Box 1686
Parkersburg, WV 26102-1686
(800) 542-9115
(304) 464-5286
FAX (304) 464-5293
Routers, tables, bits, accessories

Woodhaven
5323 W. Kimberly Rd.
Davenport, IA 52806
(800) 344-6657
(319) 391-2386
FAX (319) 391-1279
Routers, tables, bits, accessories

Woodstock International, Inc.
P.O. Box 2027
Bellingham, WA 98227
(206) 734-3482
Cast-aluminum router table

The Woodworker's Choice
1123 Industrial Drive. S.W.
Conover, NC 28613
(800) 892-4866
(704) 466-0411
FAX (704) 466-0417
Router bits

The Woodworkers' Store
21801 Industrial Blvd.
Rogers, MN 55374-9514
(800) 279-4441
(612) 428-3201
FAX (612) 428-8668
Routers, tables, bits, accessories

Woodworker's Supply
1108 North Glenn Rd.
Casper, WY 82601
(800) 645-9292
(307) 237-5528
FAX (307) 577-5272
Routers, tables, bits, accessories

INDEX

Editor: RUTH DOBSEVAGE

Designer/Layout Artist: SUZANNA M. YANNES

Illustrator: KATHLEEN RUSHTON

Photographer, except where noted: ERNIE CONOVER

Typeface: GARAMOND

Paper: FINCH OPAQUE, 70 LB., NEUTRAL pH

Printer: QUEBECOR PRINTING/HAWKINS, NEW CANTON, TENNESSEE